Early American Wars

The American Revolutionary War

New York

Robert O'Neill, Series Editor; and Daniel Marston

This edition published in 2011 by:

The Rosen Publishing Group, Inc.
29 East 21st Street
New York, NY 10010

Library of Congress Cataloging-in-Publication Data

Marston, Daniel.
The American Revolutionary War / Daniel Marston.
    p. cm.—(Early American wars)
Originally published under title: American Revolution, 1774–1783. Oxford : Osprey Pub. Ltd., 2002.
"Robert O'Neill, series editor."
Includes bibliographical references and index.
ISBN 978-1-4488-1331-5 (library binding)
    1. United States—History—Revolution, 1775–1783—Juvenile literature. 2. United States—History—Revolution, 1775–1783—Campaigns—Juvenile literature. I. O'Neill, Robert John. II. Marston, Daniel. American Revolution, 1774–1783. III. Title.
E208.M3493 2011
973.3—dc22

              2010030632

Manufactured in the United States of America

CPSIA Compliance Information: Batch #W11YA: For further information, contact Rosen Publishing, New York, New York, at 1-800-237-9932.

Copyright © 2002 Osprey Publishing Limited. First published in paperback by Osprey Publishing Limited.

On the cover: Shooting of British Brigadier Simon Fraser by American Sharpshooters, October 7, 1777. (National Archives of Canada)

Contents

Introduction

The American Revolution is rooted in a fundamental disagreement about the nature of the relationship between Great Britain and her colonial holdings in North America. At the end of the Seven Years' War, Britain, still feeling threatened by French and Spanish interests in North America, reconsidered her policies toward the Thirteen Colonies. Indifference was to give way to a more streamlined administrative policy and a greater military presence. Britain considered this necessary to safeguard both her own interests and those of her colonists, and expected that the colonies would contribute toward defraying the expenses for their own protection. Some of the colonists took a decidedly different view of the matter, considering the threat from European powers minimal and resenting an increase in military and financial focus that they viewed as intrusive and autocratic.

European powers with interests in North America were monitoring the situation closely, particularly France, Spain, and the Dutch Republic. Their interest and involvement fanned the flames of a local insurrection into a world war. When tensions flared into open insurrection, the French were quick to provide first covert and later formal military and financial aid to the American rebels. In doing so, they intended to destabilize Britain's position and advance their own interests in the area, hoping eventually to redress their recent territorial losses. Spain chose not to become directly involved, not wanting to appear as an advocate of liberty for colonial possessions in the Americas, and chose instead to ally herself with France, providing aid indirectly, also in the hope of regaining lost territory. The Dutch Republic was neutral, but benefited from the conflict by engaging in direct trade with the Thirteen Colonies, and eventually became directly involved when Great Britain declared war late in the conflict.

King George III of England. (René Chartrand)

Chronology

1775 April 19 Skirmishes at Lexington and Concord
June 17 Battle of Bunker Hill (Breed's Hill)
December 31 Battle of Quebec
1776 June 28 British attack on Fort Moultrie, Charleston, South Carolina
July 4 Declaration of Independence issued
August 27 Battle of Long Island, New York
October 28 Battle of White Plains, New York
December 8 British capture of Newport, Rhode Island
December 25–26 American surprise attack on Trenton, New Jersey
1777 January 3–4 American attack on Princeton, New Jersey
August 16 Battle of Bennington, Vermont
September 11 Battle of Brandywine, Pennsylvania
September 19 Battle of Freeman's Farm, New York
October 4 Battle of Germantown, Pennsylvania
October 7 Battle of Bemis Heights, New York
1778 February 6 Treaty of alliance signed between France and the United States (Thirteen Colonies)
June 28 Battle of Monmouth, New Jersey
July–August American siege of Newport, Rhode Island
September 7 French seize island of Dominica, West Indies
December 29 British seize Savannah, Georgia
1779 May British coastal raids, Virginia
May 8 Spain declares war on Great Britain
May–end of war Franco-Spanish siege of Gibraltar
June–September Naval stand-off, English Channel
July–August British defense of Castine, Massachusetts (Maine)

August 29–30 Battle of Newtown, New York
September–October American siege of Savannah, Georgia
1780 February–May British siege of Charleston, South Carolina
March 14 Spanish seize Mobile, Florida (Alabama)
July French forces arrive in Newport, Rhode Island
August 16 Battle of Camden, South Carolina
September 6 Battle of Pollimore, India
October 7 Battle of King's Mountain, North Carolina
December 20 Great Britain declares war on the Dutch Republic
1781 January 17 Battle of Cowpens, South Carolina
February 3 French seize St. Eustatius, West Indies
March 15 Battle of Guildford Court House, North Carolina
May 9 Fall of Pensacola, Florida
July 1 Battle of Porto Novo, India
July 6 Battle of Greenspring Farm, Virginia
August 27 Battle of Polilur, India
September 27 Battle of Sholingur, India
September 30–October 19 Franco-American siege and capture of Yorktown, Virginia
November Fall of St. Eustatius, St. Martin, and St. Bartholomew, West Indies
1782 February Fall of Minorca
February 13 French seize St. Kitts, West Indies
April 12 Battle of the Saintes, West Indies
November 30 First peace treaty signed in Paris
1783 June 13 Battle of Cuddalore, India
September 3 Peace of Paris signed

Colonial agitation

The end of the Seven Years' War in North America sparked a dispute that would eventually lead to a rebellion among the Thirteen Colonies of New Hampshire, Massachusetts, Rhode Island, Connecticut, New York, Pennsylvania, New Jersey, Delaware, Maryland, Virginia, North Carolina, South Carolina, and Georgia. The principal disagreement concerned the placement of British regulars in North America and how the British government sought to pay for their upkeep.

Britain had emerged victorious from the Seven Years' War, but in so doing had amassed a considerable debt. Before the war, the British government had undertaken minimal contact with or interference in the internal affairs of the North American colonies, aside from passing Navigation Acts that required that exports from the colonies be transported in British ships. Tensions with the French increased as the 18th century progressed, prompting the British to consider the North American colonies from a more "imperial" perspective. The government began to examine ways that the colonies could be tied into a more efficient trading system with British colonies in the Caribbean and India.

The North American theater of the Seven Years' War (more commonly known as the French-Indian War) had provided the British government with some very negative impressions. Officials had encountered considerable difficulty in gathering supplies for the war effort, and problems with locally raised colonial militia had resulted in the deployment of British regulars to the area. There has been debate over the importance of provincial militia in the French-Indian War, but there is no doubt that colonial troops could not have won the war without the support of British regulars. Some provincial

units fought well as irregular units, but others lacked the training and discipline necessary to wage a linear-style war. The discipline of the British regular was required in this theater as in all the others, and following the war's end, the British government decided that a large contingent of British regulars should be stationed permanently in North America to offset French, Spanish, and Indian ambitions in the area.

The British government settled upon a series of new taxes on the colonies as the best way to fund establishing troops in North America. The first of these was the Sugar Act of 1764. The second, the Stamp Act of 1765, charged a duty on newspapers and other official documents. This initiative provoked a negative reaction from the American colonists. Their principal grievance was that the taxes had been levied by the British Parliament, rather than by the local colonial assemblies. Popular opinion held that it was appropriate for taxation to be levied only by locally elected officials. Groups of men formed organizations known as the "Sons of Liberty" to protest the Acts. Serious rioting erupted in the colonies, to which the local British government officials felt powerless to respond, and resulted in the repeal of the Act in 1766 following a change of government in Great Britain.

The British government's next move was the Quartering Act of 1765. This was principally devised to address the supply problems that had been common during the French-Indian War, and its requirements included the provision of wagons and drivers to supply the army in the field. It was, however, the clause concerning the housing of soldiers that created problems. This provision stipulated that British regulars were to be lodged in public houses, inns, even empty homes, if barracks were overcrowded or unavailable. Furthermore, this lodging was to be at the expense of the local colonial authorities. The reaction of the Reverend John Tucker of Boston in 1768 was fairly typical: "I think we are very afflicted and in a distressed state having the Ensigns of war at our doors ... a tax laid on us to pay the exorbitant charge of providing barracks and for those undesired troops" (Doc. 973.38).

Initially this did not seem a very odious imposition, as most of the troops were to be stationed on the frontier or in territory

War in the Thirteen Colonies

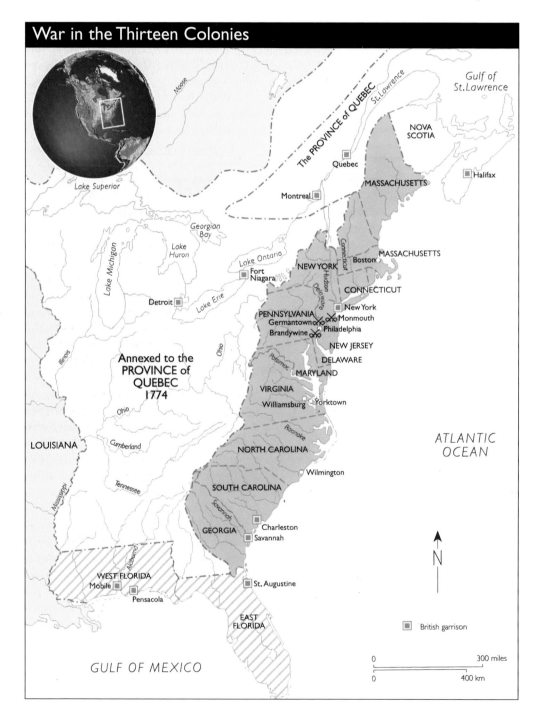

recently gained from France and Spain, such as Niagara, Crown Point, St. Augustine, Mobile, and Detroit. In practice, however, the movement of troops *en route* to their final postings was extremely disruptive. Further protest ensued, and in 1769 the colonial assemblies and the British government met to work out agreements concerning particulars of the Act, in an attempt to appease both sides. The transfer of British regulars to the Atlantic seaboard in 1770, however, strained the arrangement still further.

The Townshend Revenue Act, proposed by Chancellor of the Exchequer, Charles Townshend, was to create still more problems. This Act, passed in 1767, imposed customs duties on tea, paper, paint, glass, and lead. It sparked the ire of the colonists afresh, and assemblies from New England to the middle Atlantic expressed anger at its provisions. A Virginia militia colonel, George Washington, spoke in the Virginia House of Burgesses (Assembly) in 1769, contending that only Virginians could tax Virginians, and local merchants in most ports swore not to sell British goods or to order items from Great Britain.

Tensions rose in Boston when customs commissioners were attacked by a mob. The British government responded by dispatching 4,000 British regulars to Boston to impose control. This was a role for which regulars were not trained, and their incapability only served to incite the local population to complain of a "standing army" imposing order on a "just" civilian society. Stories of robberies and assaults by soldiers were circulated, further alienating the civilian population. Events reached a crisis on March 5, 1770, when a small contingent of British regulars, attacked by an angry mob, opened fire, killing three men and wounding five. The incident, dubbed the "Boston Massacre," was exaggerated and used as propaganda against the British. The regulars were pulled out of Boston after this episode, but tension remained.

The British government changed again in 1770, and the new Parliament, led by Frederick North, First Lord of the Treasury, repealed all duties of the Townshend Act,

John Hancock, President of the Second Continental Congress. (Ann Ronan Picture Library)

except for the duty on tea. The new government, in agreement with its predecessor, believed in its right to levy taxes upon the colonies, although Lord North did feel that this stance only hurt British merchants in the end, when their goods were boycotted in the colonies.

The next crisis arose in 1773, when Lord North imposed the Tea Act, a second tax on tea. This initiative was an attempt to boost revenue for the British East India Company. The plan was to undercut the Dutch tea supply and shift the surplus of tea to the Thirteen Colonies. Americans, however, interpreted this as a further attempt to subvert their liberty. In December 1773, a small flotilla of Company ships arrived in Boston. While docked in Boston Harbor, they were boarded in the middle of the night by a group of men, led by Samuel Adams (a political agitator) dressed as Indians. The interlopers dumped the tea into the harbor, in an act of defiance that came to be known as the Boston Tea Party.

The British government, alarmed by the situation, passed the Coercive Acts in 1774

The Boston Massacre. (Ann Ronan Picture Library)

in an attempt to restore order, especially in Boston. Lord North felt that this would be sufficient to contain the small fringe element of rebellious individuals, failing to recognize the broad base of support for some of the actions being taken. John Hancock, a prominent Boston merchant, and Samuel Adams were identified as the main troublemakers in Massachusetts. The port of Boston was closed and notice given that provincial government officials implicated in any wrongdoing could be tried in Great Britain. Lieutenant-General Thomas Gage returned to Boston with 3,500 regulars and with powers to assume the role of governor of Massachusetts. The Acts achieved the

opposite effect, provoking a negative reaction throughout the colonies.

The Quebec Act of 1774 also played a role in fomenting discontent among rebellious colonists. In an attempt to resolve the future of the French settlements of Quebec, the British government passed an Act that has had repercussions up to the present day. The colony of Quebec was allowed to keep its French language, laws, customs, and Roman Catholic religion intact, with no interference from London. Furthermore, the boundaries of the colony were extended as far west as the Mississippi, encompassing land treaties made between the British government and Indian tribes following the end of the Seven Years' War. The understanding was that the laws described in the Act would apply to this area, in recognition of the fact that many of the Indian tribes west of the mountains had been allied with France, and had thus been influenced by French customs and converted to the Catholic Church.

The Thirteen Colonies reacted strongly against the Quebec Act. Long-standing prejudice made them deeply distrustful of French Catholics, and many of the colonies resented this incursion into land west of the Appalachian Mountains, which they believed was theirs by right. They protested at being hemmed in by a Catholic colony and denied access to the rich lands to the west.

Many leading figures throughout the colonies felt that their liberties were gradually being worn away. Their dissatisfaction led to the First Continental Congress, formed in Philadelphia to discuss the Coercive Acts, the Quebec Act, and issues in Massachusetts. The First Continental Congress was convened by colonial leaders, including John Adams, George Washington, Samuel Adams, Benjamin Franklin, and Patrick Henry, with the aim of organizing

Lord Frederick North. (Bodleian Library)

General Thomas Gage.
(Anne SK Brown Collection)

It was not until July 4, 1776—after the bloodletting of 1775 and early 1776—that the Second Continental Congress, led by John Hancock, decided to declare independence from Great Britain. From this point, the Thirteen Colonies referred to themselves as "the United States of America," but as this title was not officially recognized until after the Treaty of Paris in 1783, they will continue to be referred to throughout this work as the Thirteen Colonies.

It is significant that the British government failed to recognize that the formation of the Congress indicated not just a local Massachusetts or New England rebellion, but the beginnings of a large-scale insurrection. The military situation in North America began to worsen as 1774 drew to a close. British regulars were stationed in Boston. The Quartering Act came into effect once again, increasing tension between civilians and soldiers. The delegates of the First Congress, although they considered military action a last resort, did not help the situation by calling on colonial militia to strengthen and drill more frequently. Weapons of various sizes were seized by colonists and stored away. Royal government representatives were slowly being replaced by committees who supported the conclusions of the First Continental Congress. The colonies and the British government were moving toward all-out conflict.

formal, legally recognized opposition to Parliament's actions. The Congress issued a declaration condemning the Coercive Acts as unjust and unconstitutional, and rejected the appointment of General Gage as governor. The Congress additionally addressed issues of parliamentary control over the colonies, especially with regard to taxation. At this point, the Congress was not interested in independence, merely the redress of perceived injustices.

Linear and irregular warfare

Tactics

Popular images of the American Revolution feature American "minutemen" (militia) hidden behind stone walls and trees, firing into Continental-style linear formations of British Redcoats. While this type of warfare occurred occasionally, a more accurate image would show Americans assembling for battle in linear formations opposite British forces similarly arrayed and supported by their German allies. The American Revolution had more in common with the linear warfare used in the European theaters of the Seven Years' War than with the irregular skirmishes fought on the frontiers of North America in the same conflict.

Battle of Bunker Hill. (Anne SK Brown Collection)

The flintlock musket of the Seven Years' War was still the chief weapon for all sides. The ability of an army to deploy in linear formation and maintain fire discipline was of considerable importance in training. Formations were required to march in step over open terrain, maintaining cohesion, and then deploy effectively from columns to linear formations. The British ability to accomplish this at the Battle of Monmouth saved the army from destruction, as will be described later. Following deployment in linear formation, the men were required to deliver a devastating volley against the enemy. Consistent fire discipline was crucial to the success of this maneuver.

Tactics used in the Seven Years' War also continued to be employed, particularly generals attempting to outflank their enemy

View of The ATTACK on BUNKER'S HILL, with the Burning of CHARLES TOWN, June 17. 1775.

(oblique order) when the ground permitted. The British attack at the battle of Long Island is a clear example of this tactic. Prussia's success during the Seven Years' War had inspired many armies, including the newly created American forces, the Continental Army, to emulate its firing techniques and discipline, with some success—by 1777, many Continental regiments were capable of holding their line against British and German regulars.

The American Revolution was chiefly an infantry war. The British and Continental formations deployed in ranks of men two or three deep, with artillery deployed on the flanks of battalions or regiments to mark unit boundaries. The use of only a small amount of cavalry was mainly due to practical considerations. The British encountered difficulty in transporting mounts or purchasing them in North America, and the Americans felt that the upkeep of dragoon regiments was too costly. As a result, only a few dragoon regiments were formed in the Continental Army or deployed by the British Army.

Although use of traditional methods remained constant, there were innovations in irregular warfare, following on from developments of the Seven Years' War. The British army re-employed light infantry companies in 1770–71, and by 1775–76 had begun to form these into independent battalions. The Continental Army also formed light infantry companies, and they too tended to use these in independent formations. Rifles were reintroduced for use by a small number of dedicated units. The British employed German Jäger (riflemen) and the American forces used riflemen occasionally. The numbers were small on both sides, however, and their ability to defend themselves was compromised by the amount of time it took to reload the rifle and its lack of a bayonet.

The use of combined mounted infantry/cavalry units for raiding and reconnaissance was another innovation of this period. The British began to develop this tactic in 1777 with the raising of the loyalist British Legion and Queen's Rangers corps in the New York area. These troops made a name for themselves in the later southern campaigns, with vast expanses of territory to cover. Other regiments of Jäger were occasionally formed into ad hoc mounted infantry units or attached to the Legion or Rangers, and the Americans followed suit with the mounting and use of irregular units made up of militiamen who preferred to fight in a less traditional role. The French also used mixed mounted units, the Lauzon Legion being the most famous.

Siege warfare, a significant component of the Seven Years' War, remained so in the American Revolution. Numerous battles and skirmishes were fought around fixed positions, which were dug in and defended from besieging opponents in the traditional European manner. The sieges of Savannah, Charleston, and Yorktown are classic examples.

1779 American drill book showing formation of a company and regiment and wheeling by platoons. (Anne SK Brown Collection)

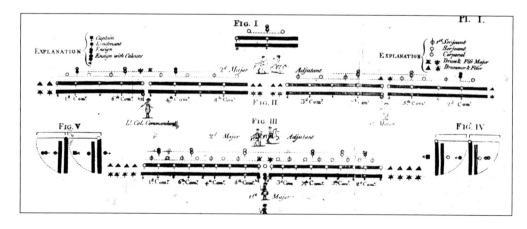

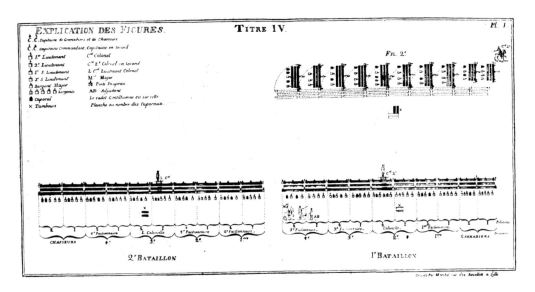

1776 French drill book showing 1st and 2nd Battalions drawn up for battle. (Anne SK Brown Collection)

The British forces

On the eve of war in 1775, the British army stood at about 48,000 officers and men, distributed throughout the garrisons of North America, Ireland, Great Britain, Minorca, Gibraltar, Africa, and the West Indies. Eight thousand of these were stationed in North America. The numbers of the overall British establishment did not increase significantly between 1775 and 1778, when only one line regiment was raised. Only the entry of the French into the war in 1778 prompted the British government to raise more regiments—nearly 30 from 1778 to 1783. This increased establishment totals to 110,000 officers and men, plus additional numbers of militia and volunteers raised to defend Great Britain.

The British Army had been successful in the Seven Years' War, but the American Revolution presented a different set of challenges. The British faced the prospect of fighting a war in hostile territory thousands of miles from their home base. Strategic planning that focused on how to end the uprising seemed to be lacking, especially during the early years of the war. British generals were unable to capitalize on tactical advantages gained after the battles of Bunker Hill and Long Island, which could potentially have crippled the military capabilities of the Americans early in the war. Infighting among

British commanders on land and sea created more problems, compounded by the arrogance of a number of British officers and government officials who considered the American forces a rabble, easily dealt with by a small force. Even if they had been capable of defeating the Americans militarily, it is questionable whether the British would have grasped how to deal with the political implications of the conflict. It is likely that they would have found themselves in the position of a garrison force attempting to contain an obstreperous political element—an unsavory prospect for any army.

The British Army consistently lacked sufficient troops to contain the insurrection, a situation made considerably worse from 1778 onward by the entry of first France and later Spain into the hostilities, forcing the British to disperse their forces throughout the world. The percentage of the British Army stationed in North America dropped from 65 percent in 1778 to only 29 percent in 1780 (Mackesy, pp. 524–25).

Despite these obstacles, the British Army itself was a formidable machine of war, a fact that was especially apparent during the conflict's early years. Its discipline and firepower generally outstripped those of the

British Light Infantryman. Artwork by Gerry Embleton. (Osprey Publishing)

surrounding marches or positions, behavior that galvanized support for the independence cause from previously neutral colonists. A French officer who was present in North America as an observer noted the following causes for British defeats up to 1777:

The present military success of the Americans can be ascribed to certain handicaps the English generals have faced: their unfamiliarity with the area of hostilities; their difficulties in obtaining reinforcements and supplies once the armies have advanced inland (Recicourt, p. 206).

The British raised a series of Loyalist Provincial Corps over the course of the war. Most of these units were trained and used as regular line infantry, with light infantry and grenadier companies. Some were used as garrison troops in outposts as remote as Charleston, in the south, or Quebec and Halifax, in Canada. Selected units were used in a more irregular role, among them Butler's Rangers, who fought alongside Indian tribes in the upstate New York and middle Atlantic regions; the majority fought in traditional Continental style.

Relatively early in the war, the British attempted to establish a centralized system for recruiting, training, and equipping the corps with the establishment of a dedicated Inspector-General, Lieutenant-Colonel Alexander Innes, in January 1777. Despite this, the British authorities demonstrated little faith in the capability of the provincial corps, and did not actively promote their raising and employment until the defeats of 1777 and the entry of the French into the conflict made the need for them apparent.

The fighting qualities of the corps ranged from excellent to poor. The British Army regulars initially disdained provincial units, but revised their opinions when reports from the field indicated competence and, in some cases, excellence. An American Establishment, not including all loyalist formations, was formed in 1779 (and formally listed in 1782), in an attempt to recognize the more successful units of loyalists and to repair damage caused by British regulars in their

American forces, and its junior officers were reliably capable under fire. These strengths were undermined, however, by the considerable problems of supply. Troops could not expect to receive adequate supplies from the local populations, which dictated dependence upon a 3,000-mile (4,800 km) supply line vulnerable to the effects of weather, privateering, and, eventually, the attentions of the French and Spanish navies.

Supply shortages meant that the British Army and its German allies engaged in frequent plunder and theft in the countryside evaluation of loyalists as second-rate. The American Establishment compromised five regiments, volunteers of Ireland, King's American Regiment, the Queen's Rangers, New York Volunteers, and British Legion. The major areas of operation for the provincial corps were in New York in 1778–79 and the southern campaigns of 1780–81. It is estimated that about 19,000 men served in the various provincial corps throughout the war.

The British authorities also utilized the services of some 10,000 Indians, chiefly from the Iroquois and Algonquin nations. They were principally employed as scouts and raiders, in recognition of their formidable knowledge of forest warfare. Their deployment sparked controversy in both America and Great Britain, and created further support for the independence movement among neutral colonists. Indians operated along the frontier regions of New York, Pennsylvania, and Virginia.

The British East India Company continued to expand and train its native forces (sepoys) in the use of traditional linear tactics following the end of the Seven Years' War. By 1775, there were about 100,000 troops in the three presidency armies of Bombay, Bengal, and Madras. Between 1778 and 1782, two Hanoverian and eight British regiments were sent to India to reinforce the East India Company forces.

The fighting qualities of the sepoys were considered to be superior. A lieutenant of the 71st Regiment of Foot noted, upon his arrival in Madras in 1780,

The Company's officers have acquired much praise by their steady adherence to the duties of their profession, which the excellent order of the sepoys clearly confirms and which strikes every stranger with surprise ... the frequent opportunities of seeing service gives them [Company troops] [a] great fund of professional knowledge (Munro, pp. 26–28).

The British and Company forces, however, lacked sufficient numbers of cavalry to contend with Haidar Ali's armies for most of this period.

Hesse-Hanau Grenadier. Artwork by Gerry Embleton. (Osprey Publishing)

German auxiliaries

The shortfall in British regular forces compelled the British to seek a loan of troops from Russia. The Russians refused to loan troops for service in North America, and Britain was forced to look elsewhere. Having used troops from the German princely states before, she made use of this resource again, and troops from Hanover were sent to Minorca and Gibraltar to release British troops for North American service.

(Troops from Hanover were not considered mercenaries, since one of George III's titles was Elector of Hanover.) By early 1776, the British had negotiated treaties with Brunswick, Hesse-Cassel, Hesse-Hanu, Anspach, Waldeck, and Anhalt for troops for the war in America. Since the largest contingent came from Hesse-Cassel, all German auxiliaries were commonly referred to as Hessians.

Over the course of the war 29,166 German auxiliaries served in North America (Fletcher, p. 63). Most of the German troops were organized in traditional Continental style. The grenadier companies were often formed into independent units, and there was also a *Jäger* corps, which was in great demand after the battle of Long Island. The *Jäger* corps averaged 700 men throughout the war.

The German auxiliaries caused considerable problems for the British, principally with discipline and public relations. The German troops became known for pillaging and destroying farms and houses in 1776. While all factions were guilty of this, the Americans used the German abuses as propaganda, and the French officer von Closen noted "the ravages of the Hessians who made themselves hated by their lack of discipline and inconsideration for the peaceful inhabitants during the winter quarters in New Jersey" (Closen, p. 115).

The fighting qualities of the German contingents, like those of the provincial corps, ranged from excellent to poor. A French officer commented that "the English, Hessian, and Anspach troops, [were] the elite of those who had been in Carolina" (Rice and Brown, Vol. I, p. 151). The Hessian troops were considered the equal of the Prussian Army, and the *Jäger* corps was held in high esteem by the American and French forces arrayed against it. The Brunswick contingent, on the other hand, which served in Burgoyne's campaign of 1777, was not so highly regarded; although well-disciplined, their fighting abilities were considered mediocre. Troops from Hesse-Hanau were criticized by Lieutenant-General Frederick Haldimand, the British commander in

Canada in 1778, as being unfit for the American war.

The fact that German troops were used as part of the British Army in North America caused great consternation amongst the American colonial population and like-minded individuals in Great Britain. Their presence has historically been given as a reason why the American people dislike and distrust mercenaries. This is a simplistic and somewhat hypocritical argument, especially considering that the American commanders apparently had no qualms about accepting the services of various soldiers of fortune from Europe.

The numbers of European troops serving with the American forces did not reach the levels of the German auxiliaries. Some of the officers, however, notably Frederick William Augustus, Baron von Steuben, and Gilbert Mottier, Marquis de Lafayette, played instrumental roles in the development of the Continental Army and were accordingly awarded high-ranking positions. There were small "foreign" corps in the American forces, including Pulaski's Legion, Von Heer's Provost Corps, and Brigadier-General Charles Tuffin Armand's Independent Chasseurs.

Additionally, once the French officially entered the war as allies of the Americans, the French forces employed considerable numbers of mercenary troops within their ranks. Nearly one-fifth of the French Army in France and overseas was made up of foreign troops; the famous Lauzon Legion, which served with distinction in the American colonies, was made up of foreigners whose word of command was German.

The American forces

The Americans began the war without a proper army. The troops arrayed against the British in the spring of 1775 consisted of partially trained militia. The Militia Law of 1775 designated all free men between the ages of 16 and 50 as liable for duty, and each colony formed its own militia into companies and regiments.

Private, 4th Massachusetts Regiment. Artwork by Bill Younghusband. (Osprey Publishing)

countrymen. As General George Washington pointed out:

Men just dragged from the tender scene of domestic life; unaccustomed to the din of arms; totally unaccustomed with any kind of military skill . . . when opposed to troops regularly trained and disciplined and appointed supreme in arms makes them timid and ready to fly from their shadows (Weigley, p. 5).

The militia had some successes during the war against regular troops, but on the whole lacked sufficient discipline or training to undertake combat on a European-style battlefield.

There were also benefits to the colonists' ability to muster a pro-independence militia. Militia could be used to offset any loyalist attempts to provide support for the British effort; and, when used in a more irregular role, especially in raids and defense, the militia often exceeded expectations. Following the Battle of King's Mountain, 1780, an American Major-General noted:

This battle as well as many others under Generals Sumter, Marion, and others, proves that militia are brave men, and will fight if you let them come to action in their own way. There are very few actions when they are drawn up in line of battle, that they could be brought to stand and reserve their fire until the enemy came near enough (Moultrie, Vol. II, p. 244).

A French officer,Sublieutenant Jean Baptiste Antoine de Verger, observed that "they [the militia] give occasional examples of bravery when they are superior in numbers or when in possession of some defile the enemy must pass through, into which they can fire from ambush" (Rice and Brown, Vol. I, p. 152).

The need for properly trained professional soldiers prompted the Continental Congress to sanction the formation of the Continental Army, despite widespread American bias against a standing army dating back to the English Civil Wars. The proposed structure divided American forces between the militia

The greatest problem with the militia organization was that there was no regular training schedule. When training was organized, the men were called to arms for a specific period of time, usually only 30–60 days, and then returned to their families. The militia was not considered fit to take on British regulars, even by their own

General George Washington. (Anne SK Brown Collection)

of the colonies and the regular Continental Army. Shortages of men available for the Continentals necessitated the use of militia in a supporting role to Continental operations, and as drafts for the Continental Army. The drill master, Prussian Captain (later American Major-General) Frederick Augustus, Baron von Steuben, described the plans for militia in 1779 thus: "Our business is now to find out the means of rendering that militia capable to supply the want of a well regulated standing army at least as much as lies in our power" (Boston Public Library, Ch.F.7.78).

The first attempts at organizing a professional army were undertaken in the summer of 1775. The "Separate Army" was formed in upstate New York in June. The Continental Congress in Philadelphia also sanctioned the formation of troops outside Boston to be listed as a Continental Force or the "New England Army." On July 2, 1775, George Washington was named Commander-in-Chief of all Continental and militia forces serving under the auspices of the Army of the United Colonies, both existing and to be raised. He inherited a force of some 17,000 men, mostly from the New England colonies. All of the units had different establishments, making standardization difficult. Most of the army was relieved of duty by the end of 1775, leaving Washington to muster another round of troops for the 1776 campaign. This army, again, was disbanded at the end of 1776 when its enlistment contracts ended.

Eventually the Continental Congress called for the formation of the Continental Army on September 26, 1776. The American defeats of 1776 had made Congress realize that a well-trained body of men was needed, and that one-year contracts were not sufficient to prepare troops to face the British in battle. As a Hessian General noted: "General Washington and Putnam are praised by friend and foe alike, but all their mastery in war will be of no avail with a mob of conscripted undisciplined troops" (*Revolution in America*, p. 40).

The new army was to have 88 regiments (battalions) formed from each of the Thirteen Colonies. The great difference between this force and previous musters was that the new army was to be raised for three years, or for the duration of the war, whichever was shorter. The three-year limitation on enlistment was imposed in response to recruits' unwillingness to join for an unknown duration. The Continental Army's authorized strength was 75,000 men, which it never attained. The highest level of recruitment ever reached was 18,000, in October 1778.

The Continental Army was divided among three major armies, the Northern (Separate), Main, and Southern armies, each of which took on different numbers of battalions over the course of the war. The Continental Army consistently encountered problems in providing enough men and supplies. It was forced to compete against recruiters for the colonial militia to assemble sufficient troops, and conscription was periodically employed in an attempt to fill the army's ranks. During 1777, many commanders had difficulty clothing and arming the men in their regiments, and even in friendly territory it was difficult to supply enough food. Pay was also a considerable problem, as the paper money used to pay troops and officers dropped steadily in value during the course of the war. Even facing severe shortages of supplies, men, and officers, however, the Continental Army was still able to form for battle year after year. The British were unable to completely destroy it, and on more than one occasion were defeated by the combined force of Continental and militia troops.

There is a debate among historians as to whether the Continental Army represented a levy of supporters of the independence movement, or its members had more in common with their European counterparts— men who joined the army only for payment and signing bonuses. Some contend that the militia of the time represented a more politicized element of the American forces. One historian noted that "there was little commitment among the American rank and file to the constitutional cause of Independence and very few of our patriots chose to re-enlist for a second or third time" (Duffy, p. 285).

It is still debatable whether the Continentals were a "republican" army or a purely professional force with no concern for political issues, but ultimately they performed well in the field and proved themselves to their European allies. A French officer commented:

I admire the American troops tremendously! It is indescribable that soldiers composed of men of every age, even of children of fifteen, of whites and blacks, almost naked, unpaid and rather poorly fed, can march so well and withstand fire so steadfastly (Closen, p. 102).

In developing tactical training, the Continental Army had several sources of information available. Some of the senior generals appointed had seen service in British units during the Seven Years' War. Their experience was bolstered by input from a series of foreign officers who had come to advise the army and to seek adventure. They came from Prussia, Poland, France, and other European states. This infusion of officers caused confusion in the American chain of command but also provided significant expertise in organization and tactics.

The Continental Army drew up its own tactical manuals, which were largely based upon contemporary British documents. Major-General von Steuben spent the winter of 1777–78 drilling the Continental Army along Prussian military lines. He also regulated the size of battalions and standardized a specific drill to be followed by all units of the Continental Army.

In 1781, there was further organizational streamlining, partially because a number of regiments were being disbanded due to lack of manpower. The fighting capabilities of the American forces remained fairly strong despite this; members of the French contingent commented on the American forces upon arrival in Newport, Rhode Island, in 1780. Sublieutentant de Verger noted that:

The American Continental troops are very war-wise and quite well disciplined. They are thoroughly inured to hardship, which they endure with little complaint so long as their officers set them an example, but it is imperative the officers equal their troops in firmness and resolution (Rice and Brown, Vol. I, p. 152).

Another significant asset for the Continental Army was its understanding of the need for small reforms within the organization. A French officer, Lieutenant-Colonel Jean Baptiste Tennant of Pulaski's Legion, wrote an important paper examining army structure. It appears to originate after 1779, when the original commander of Pulaski's Legion was killed and succeeded by Lieutenant-Colonel Tennant. The paper, called "Uniformity Among American Troops," outlined "a scheme for establishing uniformity in the services, discipline, manoeuvre of formations of troops in the armies of the United States" (Boston Public Library, Ch.F.8.55a).

Tennant proposed innovations designed to accommodate the specific needs of the Continental Army. Pointing out that the army, unlike its European counterparts, did not have the benefit of large cadres of men and officers with years of military experience, he stressed that to compensate:

The manoeuvres to be introduced must be as simple as possible. The chief objectives are for the officers to know how to lead their platoons and keep their men together and for the soldiers to keep rank and file ... that all manoeuvres be performed ... in greatest silence (Boston Public Library, Ch.F.8.55a).

He also recommended the appointment of an Inspector General to formulate training throughout the army, but stipulated that:

Before introducing any new thing the Inspector General is to propose it to the Commander-in-Chief in the field ... neither the Inspector General nor inspectors of any other detached army shall be authorized to give a general order without previously communicating it with the Commander-in-Chief for his approbility [approval] (Boston Public Library, Ch.F.8.55a).

The French forces

The French Army had emerged from the Seven Years' War at a low point, having been defeated in North America, Europe, and India. Evaluation of its performance had brought about a number of reforms from 1763 to 1775. Artillery units were revamped and standardized into seven large regiments, and infantry regiments were regularized as well. By 1776, all regiments comprised two battalions, with each battalion composed of one grenadier, one chasseur (light infantry), and four fusilier companies.

The training of the infantry and cavalry was standardized and revamped to include summer training camps. The Crown undertook to supply the regiments directly with clothing and muskets to counteract the officers' practice of profiting on military supply contracts. Military enlistment was fixed at eight years, to provide a large corps of properly trained soldiers. By 1778, there were more than 200,000 men in the French Army. The French Army had no continental commitments during the war, as it had in the Seven Years' War, and was therefore able to direct most of its energies against British interests throughout the world.

The performances of the French Army at Yorktown and in the West Indies demonstrated the successes of the reforms and presented a different army from the one that the British had fought in the Seven Years' War. A French expeditionary force arrived at Newport in 1780, under the command of Lieutenant-General Jean de Vimeur, Comte de Rochambeau. Thomas McKean of the Continental Congress reviewed the troops in Philadelphia and afterward wrote to Rochambeau:

The brilliant appearance and exact discipline of the several Corps do the highest honor to their

French officer of the Armagnac Regiment. (Canadian Parks Services)

officers, and to afford a happy presage of the most distinguished services in a cause which they have so zealously espoused (Rice and Brown, Vol. I, p. 46 footnote 72).

Shot heard round the world

The year 1775 marked the formal outbreak of hostilities between the British and Americans. A small skirmish in Lexington led to a larger confrontation in Concord, and the British withdrawal from Concord sparked a savage fight for survival and the beginning of outright conflict. The battle of Breed's Hill (Bunker Hill), in June, was the first pitched battle of the war. This was followed by a bold American attempt, in December 1775, to seize and conquer Canada. After these events, there could be no turning back. It was war.

The armed struggle for America began on April 19, 1775, in the towns of Lexington and Concord, Massachusetts. It could easily have been sooner. By late 1774, the British government was growing tired of its contentious North American colonists. General Gage, Commander-in-Chief in North America, received orders in December to arrest the instigators, but he considered the number of British troops available locally too small to be effective. Most of the British forces in North America were gathered and sent to Boston, nearly 13 battalions of infantry by the spring of 1775. Gage still considered this inadequate to deal with a possible insurrection.

In early April, Gage received reports that a large cache of weapons and gunpowder was being stored at Concord, 16 miles (26 km) northwest of Boston. The local militia was aware that the British knew about the stores, but not when the British might move against it. Senior members of the Continental Congress, such as John Adams and John Hancock, were in Lexington, and there was fear that the British would move to arrest them.

On April 18 at 8:00 PM, the commanding officers of the British regiments in Boston were ordered to send their light and grenadier companies to the beach near the Magazine Guard by 10:00 PM. These troops numbered between 600 and 700 men and were commanded by Lieutenant-Colonel Francis Smith of the 10th Foot and Major John Pitcairn of the Marines. The troops were ferried across the Charles River toward Cambridge. All of the troops landed on Cambridge Marsh by midnight, but had to wait till 2:00 AM before moving, in order to allow the shipping and unloading of provisions to be completed. Lieutenant Barker noted, "Few but the commanding officers knew what expedition we were going upon" (Barker, p. 31). Paul Revere and William Dawes secretly left Boston and rode toward Lexington and Concord to raise the alarm that the British were marching on the stores.

As the British troops marched toward Lexington, they began to receive intelligence that a large group of armed men was forming near the common at Lexington. Lieutenant-Colonel Smith sent a messenger back to Boston for reinforcements. A reinforcement brigade was ordered ready to move from Boston overland to Lexington. Due to orders not being conveyed correctly and time wasted to correct the mistake, the brigade was delayed and did not march until 8:45 AM (Mackenzie, p. 19). The Lexington militia formed a company of 70 men on Lexington Green, under the command of Captain John Parker, a veteran of the Seven Years' War.

Major Pitcairn and his companies arrived at Lexington Green just as the militia was forming up at around 6:00 AM. Major Pitcairn called upon the militia to lay down their arms and return to their homes. The American commander, Parker, told his men not to fire; the British moved forward and a shot was fired. There has been extensive debate about who actually fired the first shot. Lieutenant Barker contends that "on our coming near them they [the American

Tarring and feathering a British official. (Ann Ronan Picture Library)

militia] fired one or two shots" (Barker, p. 32). The situation was confusing for both sides, and Barker mentions that, after the initial shots, "our men without any orders rushed in upon them, fired, and put them to flight" (Barker, p. 32). The firing lasted for 15–20 minutes, when Pitcairn managed to restore order. Eight militiamen lay dead and 10 more were wounded. The British had suffered one wounded man.

Following this engagement, Pitcairn and the light infantry moved on to Concord to destroy the cache of weapons. The militia surrounding Concord was mobilized and moved to intercept the British column. The British seized Concord, and the light infantry was sent to secure bridges north and south of town, while the grenadiers dealt with destroying the weapons and gunpowder in the area. A fight broke out at the North Bridge after the British had occupied both sides. As the militia moved forward, the British withdrew from one side and fired a volley into the militia. An American stated that "we were all ordered to load [muskets] and had strick [strict] orders not to fire till they fired first, then to fire as fast as we could ... the British ... fired three guns one after another ... we then was all ordered to fire ... and not to kill our own men" (Barrett, p. 10). The Concord militia opened fire and according to a British officer, "the weight of their fire was such that we were obliged to give way" (Lister, p. 27).

The British suffered one killed and 11 wounded, including four officers. They withdrew toward Concord, and orders were received at around midday for all units to fall back toward Boston, the military stores having been destroyed. As the troops left Concord, sniping began from houses along the road to Boston. About one mile (2 km) outside of Concord, the British column crossed at Meriam's Corner, where it became bunched up. Militiamen opened up on the large column, inflicting heavy casualties on the flanks and rear.

The relieving brigade from Boston met up with the remainder of the British column at Lexington, bringing the numbers of British troops close to 1,500 men. The combined force marched out toward Boston. As a British officer noted: "We were attacked on all sides from woods, and orchards and from stone walls and from every house on the road side" (Evelyn, p. 54). The British reaction to this sort of attack was described as follows: "The soldiers were so enraged at suffering from an unseen enemy, that they forced open many a house from which the fire proceeded, and put to death all those found in them" (Mackenzie, pp. 20–21). Militiamen poured in from all the surrounding towns to fight against the withdrawing British column, but the British were able to keep them at a distance with the use of flanking parties and a very good rearguard formation.

When they arrived in Cambridge, the British column decided to head toward Charlestown, as the bridge from Cambridge to Boston had either been destroyed or was heavily defended. The column arrived at Charlestown at 7:00 PM and occupied the area until boats were sent to ferry the troops back over to Boston. The militia did not pursue the British into Charlestown because the area was open terrain. As Barker noted: "The rebels did not chuse [sic] to follow us to the Hill as they must have fought us on open ground and that they did not like" (Barker, p. 36).

The British lost about 70 killed and 170 wounded during the day's fighting, while the Americans are estimated to have lost 100 men killed and wounded. The British had been successful in extricating themselves from the area and had applied good light infantry tactics in clearing the militia from the stone walls and houses that lined the road to Boston.

Bunker Hill

Following this first skirmish, the surrounding colonies sent militia reinforcements to Boston during the remainder of April and May. By the end of May, militia numbers had swelled to about 17,000 men. The British received reinforcements in the shape of

Major-Generals (later Lieutenant-Generals) Sir William Howe, Sir Henry Clinton, and Sir John Burgoyne, as well as the 35th, 49th, and 63rd Regiments of Foot over the course of May and June. Gage finally felt equipped to occupy the two dominant heights commanding Boston, Dorchester Heights and Charlestown (Breed's Hill). The rebels received word of this and began to dig a redoubt on Breed's Hill on the evening of June 16, 1775.

The British decided to attack the American positions on Breed's Hill, in an episode that has come down the years of history as the Battle of Bunker Hill. Colonel William Prescott was in charge of the American forces on the hill; these were estimated at a few thousand men. Defensive positions had been dug from the redoubt down to the Mystic River in an attempt to rebuff any flanking attack from the British.

The British sent a force of 2,000 men over to Charlestown in the early afternoon of June 17, under the command of General Howe. Howe, a veteran of the French-Indian War, understood the needs of light infantry and the difficulties of assailing a fixed position frontally, so it is even more surprising that his main attack was a frontal assault. This can perhaps be attributed to the arrogant belief that the rebels would flee once they saw the British regulars advancing.

The British left, under the command of Brigadier Robert Pigott, had marched to within yards of the American lines when a heavy volley was fired into their midst. A second volley followed, forcing the left wing to fall back. The British troops were supported by artillery, but this had no impact on the first attack. One American observer described "the balls flying almost as thick as hailstones from the ships and floating batteries . . . our people stood the fire some time" (Haskell, p. 273). Howe's troops on the right flank were similarly unable to breach the American defenses. Pigott launched a second frontal attack with no more success. A British officer said, "The oldest soldiers here [Boston] say that it was the hottest fire they ever saw, not even the

Battle of Minden [1759] . . . was equal to it" (Balderston and Syrett, p. 33). Howe's second attempt on the right wing failed as well.

Reinforcements arrived as the decision was made to attempt a third and final attack. The American defenders, meanwhile, were running low on ammunition, and Prescott ordered his men to hold their fire until the last possible moment. The British line advanced, and when they were within 30–60 feet (9–18 m), the Americans fired their last rounds. The British pushed forward with bayonets fixed, driving the Americans from their positions. The Americans managed to retreat over the Charlestown Neck without much opposition, however, as Gage failed to translate the victory into a decisive rout.

The British had seized the hill, but it was a Pyhrric victory. Of the 2,500 British troops involved, 228 had been killed and 800 wounded. The Americans, on the other hand, had lost only 100 killed and 270 wounded. These casualties were the worst the British suffered during the war. As Gage noted in a letter that was published in the *London Gazette*, "The tryals [sic] we have shew that the Rebels are not the despicable Rabble too many have supposed them to be" (July 22–25, 1775). This battle also made clear to the Americans that, though they might be successful in defense, they would require a professional Continental-style army to challenge the British in the open fields of America.

After the casualties suffered at Breed's Hill, the British decided not to attack Dorchester Heights. While Charlestown was occupied, the British remained holed up in Boston for the rest of the year. General Gage was replaced by General Sir William Howe as Commander-in-Chief of America in October 1775.

Battle of Quebec

The final military campaign of 1775 took place in upstate New York and Canada. American forces had seized the British posts at Fort Ticonderoga and Crown Point in May

1775. In June, the Continental Congress created the Separate Army, giving the command to Major-General Philip Schuyler, along with orders to attack Canada. Schuyler's deputy, Brigadier Richard Montgomery, a former British regular, was given field command of the army. He was ordered to attack toward Montreal and rendezvous with a New England force under the command of Brigadier Benedict Arnold. Arnold's force followed the Penobscot River (in present-day Maine), intending to arrive outside Quebec City, the principal British garrison in Canada.

and arrived fatigued and hungry outside Quebec in mid-November. Montgomery arrived in early December. The British commander and governor at Quebec, Lieutenant-General Sir Guy Carleton, had only 1,800 troops, nearly all of whom were newly raised militia or recruits. Most of the regulars had been sent to Boston.

The Americans fielded about 1,000 men. They attacked the city on December 31, one day before many of Arnold's New England troops' terms of enlistment ended. A snowstorm began as the attack was launched; an American soldier described the scene:

This morning about 4 AM, the time appointed to storm the city, our army divided into different parts to attack the city ... we got near the walls when a heavy fire of cannon and small arms began from the enemy, they being prepared and expecting us that night ... came to the wall cannon roaring like thunder and musket balls flying like hail (Haskell, 1/1776).

Brigadier Montgomery was killed and General Arnold wounded. The Americans suffered heavy losses, and, though they remained outside the city, the threat to Quebec had passed.

The British strategy of 1775 had been to apply overt military action to try to resolve a problem that was essentially political in origin. Their aim in doing so was to quell the growing dissatisfaction of the colonists and in this they failed. The concentration of British regulars in Boston had not frightened the local population into submission. On the contrary, the population had become more openly hostile in the presence of troops. The attempt to seize and destroy the weapon caches in Concord, while technically successful, had sparked an all-out rebellion. Lack of strategic planning found the bulk of the British North American forces hemmed into Boston, surrounded by a hostile citizenry. The victory at Breed's Hill, won at such great cost, had left the senior commanders

Montgomery's advance went according to plan, but the British and Canadian militiamen at St. John's, Quebec, unexpectedly held out for five weeks. Montreal fell on November 13, 1775, with cold weather setting in. Arnold's force had underestimated crossing the Maine frontier,

Lieutenant General Sir William Howe.
(Anne SK Brown Collection)

in Boston hesitant to destroy the local American forces surrounding them.

Finally, the Americans had almost succeeded in capturing Canada. While an American victory would almost certainly have provoked a more definitive response from the British, the reality remained that the Americans had successfully invaded as far as Quebec, conclusively demonstrating just how vulnerable the British were in dealing with the insurrection. Senior members of the British government called for a naval blockade of the colonies, but the ultimate decision was to concentrate resources in a land war.

The Americans had been able to achieve great things in 1775. They had forced the British into Boston and kept them trapped there. Some members of the Continental Congress recognized, however, that the British were not going to give in easily and stressed the need for proper military training and force to counter the British regulars.

Colonial and world war

This chapter will deal with the two distinct theaters of the American Revolution: the land war and the sea war. First, an overall history of the war at sea will cover 1775–83 and the chief engagements of the various navies. Naval engagements that directly affect land operations will be dealt with alongside the relevant land campaign.

The land war in North America encompassed a large area, involving the interests of numerous colonial powers, and the incursions of France, Spain, and the Dutch Republic in 1778, 1779, and 1780, respectively, gave the war a more global character. For this reason, the account of the land war will be divided into subheadings covering years and areas of operation. The war in North America will be divided into the northern campaign, encompassing New England, upstate New York, and Canada. The middle Atlantic campaign will focus on operations in lower New York, New Jersey, and Pennsylvania. The southern campaign will cover the operations from Virginia to Georgia. From 1778 onwards, an additional subheading entitled "Outside the Thirteen Colonies" will be included. This section will consider the British, French, Spanish, and later Dutch engagements in Florida, the West Indies, Europe (Minorca, Gibraltar, and the English Channel), and India. There was also some fighting on the West African coast, but this was relatively minor and will not be discussed due to space considerations.

The naval war: 1775–83

The main naval engagements of the American Revolution were between France and Great Britain, although the Spanish fleet entered the fray in 1779, tipping the balance in France's favor. The Royal Navy spent most of the war period on the defensive, and the French Navy, though able to grapple with the Royal Navy, was unable to decisively cripple the opposition and bring the naval conflict to a close. The naval war was characterized by local victories, undermined by the failure of the commanders to capitalize on their successes. Only a few engagements influenced the land campaigns in any way, although the naval forces were instrumental in transporting and landing ground forces in North America, the West Indies, and India.

The most important component of each navy was its ships of the line. The naval term "ship of the line" refers to three-masted, square-rigged vessels carrying 60 or more cannon on board (the minimum firepower to be able to stand in the "line" of battle against an enemy). Ships with fewer than 60 cannon were referred to as cruisers and frigates. First-rate ships carried 90–100 guns; second-rate usually fielded 80–90 guns; third-rate ships had 64–74 guns. Fourth-rate ships (frigates) usually carried 50 guns, and fifth- and sixth-rate ships (cruisers) carried 24–40 guns.

The Royal Navy North American Squadron, under the command of Admiral Lord Howe, spent 1775–78 concentrating on three major naval efforts: supply and reinforcement of the British Army; blockade of the American coast; and raids on strategic points along the coastline. The entry of the French into the hostilities in 1778 committed the Royal Navy to a world war destined to stretch its resources very thin. The Royal Navy did not follow the strategy successfully employed in the Seven Years' War and attempt to blockade the French Navy in its chief ports of Toulon and Brest. Instead, efforts were principally focused on protecting the West Indies and British home waters, with smaller deployments in North America and the Indian Ocean. In 1778, there were 41 ships stationed in North America, and eight ships in the West Indies. By 1780, the numbers had been effectively reversed, with 13 ships in North America and 41 in the West Indies (Conway, p. 158).

As with the British Army, the Royal Navy was not committed to a serious building program until the threat of French opposition became a reality. As of July 1, 1778, the Royal Navy stood as follows: 66 ships of the line—30 in European waters, 14 in North America, 13 *en route* to North America, and the rest serving in or *en route* to Minorca and India (Dull, *French Navy* p. 359). By 1782, the Royal Navy's strength had increased to 94 ships of the line but did not outnumber the combined strength of the Spanish and French fleets, at 54 and 73 ships respectively (Dull, *French Navy* pp. 363–365).

Tactics also remained largely unchanged; Royal Navy commanders had been given "Fighting Instructions" that tied them rigidly to "line-ahead" tactics. The line-ahead was similar to linear formations of the land armies. The idea was for a squadron to form in line and attack the enemy fleet with broadside fire along a continuous line, hoping for a break in the enemy's lines of ships. Many commanders did not follow this system, however, choosing instead to attempt the "melee." The melee, or penetration of the enemy's line of ships, was intended to inflict damage by more aggressive means. Some commanders were brought before court martial for deliberate use of the melee, but most were exonerated, reflecting the opinion of the courts martial that battle tactics should be decided by the commander at sea.

The French Navy had emerged from the Seven Years' War with a poor reputation and immediately set to work to reform the service. New ships were built, naval officers considered unfit to command were relieved of duty, naval artillery was improved, and, most important, training was established as a

priority. Two major naval works devised and implemented were the "Tactique Nava" and "Les Manoeuvres," both of which were considered to be superior to the British "Fighting Instructions." The absence of a Continental threat to France led to the decision to combat the Royal Navy on the high seas from the European theater to India and the West Indies. On July 1, 1778, the French Navy stood at 52 ships of the line; 32 ships were stationed in European waters, with 12 ships *en route* to North America and the rest in the Mediterranean and Indian oceans (Dull, *French Navy* p. 359).

The Spanish fleet also played an important role in the war on the high seas. On July 1, 1779, the Spanish fleet stood at 58 ships of the line. The vast majority of the Spanish ships were stationed in European waters and Gibraltar, with smaller squadrons in the New World (Dull, *French Navy* p. 361). The Spanish ships were very well designed and some naval historians considered them superior to both their French and British counterparts. Unfortunately, the Spanish Navy lacked a well-trained officer and ratings corps to man the ships, and neither the tactics nor the professionalism of the Spanish Navy was equivalent to those of the French and British.

In the autumn of 1775, the Continental Congress authorized the construction of a small American fleet, consisting of only five ships. The Continental Navy and the recently raised Continental marines captured the Bahamas Islands from the British in 1776, marking the first combined American naval-marine operations. The Continental Navy was successful in raiding parts of Nova Scotia and even parts of the British coast, but was never strong enough to cause real damage to the Royal Navy. The serious threat to the British came from the privateering activities of the Continental Navy and commercial fleets. Development of an American Navy ceased after the French joined the American effort.

The first significant engagement between the French and British navies took place on

July 27, 1778, off the coast of Brittany. The British squadron, under the command of Admiral Lord Augustus Keppel, engaged a French squadron under the command of Admiral Comte d'Orvilliers. The French force was able to slip back to Brest. Both sides suffered damage but the battle decided nothing. The rest of the engagements recounted here were those considered locally decisive.

In January 1780, Admiral Sir George Brydges Rodney and a squadron of ships left Great Britain with provisions and stores for Gibraltar. On January 16, his squadron fought an engagement with a Spanish squadron under the command of Don Juan de Langara. One of the Spanish ships was destroyed and another six were captured. The Spanish squadron blockading Gibraltar was easily dispersed and Rodney was able to lift the siege. Rodney and his squadron sailed for the West Indies, where they engaged a French squadron commanded by Comte de

French ships of the line. (Library of Congress)

Guichen on April 17 and May 15, 1780. The French ships were damaged, but Rodney was unable to completely destroy the squadron, only to delay its landing in the West Indies. In September 1781, squadrons under the command of Rear Admiral Thomas Graves and Comte de Grasse met off Chesapeake Bay Capes. De Grasse had sailed from the West Indies with reinforcements for the French forces in North America and 24 ships of the line. He was able to land his troops unmolested. Admiral Graves sailed with 19 ships of the line, drawing from the West Indies and North American squadrons. The two squadrons engaged for more than two hours, with both sides suffering heavy damage. For the next two days each side watched the other, but following reports of a larger French squadron on the way, the British naval high command decided to withdraw to New York. This decision meant, incidentally, that British troops at Yorktown could not be reinforced, which sealed their fate. This is discussed in more detail later.

In April 1782, the main West Indies squadrons of the British and French navies met off the coast of Dominica and Guadeloupe. The French flotilla, under the command of de Grasse, had sailed for Jamaica with an invasion force of 10,000 troops. The British combined squadrons, under the command of Rodney and Rear-Admiral Samuel Hood, chased de Grasse. During the engagement, Rodney was able to smash through the French lines with a mêlée attack. Five French ships were taken in the battle of the Saintes, but Rodney failed to pursue the remainder of the French line. Admiral Hood criticized him for this action, but it did stave off the invasion of Jamaica and so is considered a decisive engagement.

The Royal Navy was uncontested in the East Indies between 1778 and 1781. The French admiralty did not wish to engage the Royal Navy until 1782. From then the British commander, Rear-Admiral Sir Edward Hughes, engaged a French squadron under the command of Admiral Pierre-Andre Suffren de Saint-Tropez five times in two years. The French were victors in all the engagements, but, like the Royal Navy, they were unable to capitalize on their advantage. The British were therefore able to hold on to their gains in India and the Indian Ocean.

The land war: 1776

The spring of 1776 marked further moves toward America's political independence from Great Britain. The fighting of the previous year and the raiding and burning of towns by the Royal Navy had pushed the American colonies beyond the reach of conciliation and closer to cutting their ties conclusively. The colonial governments were authorizing the use of privateers, war against loyalists, opening of trade with European nations, and the embargo of British goods. After much wrangling over terms and conditions, the Thirteen Colonies declared political independence from Great Britain on July 4, 1776, and recreated themselves the "Thirteen United States of America."

The political and social implications of the Declaration of Independence have been debated for decades and fall outside the scope of this work, except to say that this act galvanized some elements of society and alienated others, particularly those who considered themselves neutral on the question. Citizens who wanted outright independence felt that the Declaration of Independence was the last step toward that independence. The second Continental Congress had finally and formally decided. However, some people who sympathized with the original grievances felt that the Declaration of Independence had gone too far. They did not want to sever ties with Britain.

The effect on the Continental Army appeared to be positive. An American colonel commented that:

The Declaration of Independence ... was announced to the army in general orders, and filled everyone with enthusiastic zeal, as the point was now forever settled, and there was no further hope of reconciliation and dependence on the mother country (Tallmadge, p. 9).

Such a state of affairs also made a clear distinction between loyalists and American republicans, a situation that provoked a violent civil war among the civilians of North America.

The British had a strategy in place for the 1776 campaign season. Lord George Germain was the Secretary of State for the American Colonies from November 1775 to February 1782. He was a former military officer and

his role was to coordinate military and political strategy with the British commanders in America. Its first component was the British Northern Army. This group, under the command of Major- (later Lieutenant-) General Sir John Burgoyne, was to sail for Quebec to lift the siege, then transfer command to General Carleton to clear Canada of American forces, and strike south toward the Hudson River. A second contingent, leaving from Halifax under the command of General Howe, would attack

Declaration of Independence. (The British Museum)

Lord George Germain. (René Chartrand)

the New York and Long Island region and link up with Carleton coming from the north. The intention was to cut off New England from the rest of the colonies, leaving it to "rot" under a Royal Navy blockade. A third and smaller expedition was to attack Charleston in the south.

Northern campaign

During the winter months of 1775–76, the British troops in Boston were hemmed in on three sides. General Howe refused to fight Washington and the New England Army, preferring to wait for reinforcements. Howe was unaware that the New England Army that surrounded him was at times barely capable of offering resistance as it tried to cope with ongoing problems of desertion and re-enlistment. General Washington had artillery captured from Fort Ticonderoga placed on Dorchester Heights, and by early March 1776 the guns were in place and firing upon the British in Boston. Howe ordered an attack to take place, but had to cancel the order on account of inclement weather. Howe then decided to evacuate Boston, and did so on March 17, 1776. The British officer Kemble recorded: "Troops ordered to embark at 5 in the morning and completed by 8 and under sail by 9" (Kemble, p. 73). The British force sailed from Boston for Halifax, Howe considering that his troops needed rest and refitting before heading toward their next battle in New York.

In Canada, the British relieving force arrived outside Quebec on May 6. The Americans lifted the siege and fell back toward Montreal, while the British pushed toward Trois-Rivières. The American Army had suffered from smallpox and low morale over the course of winter 1775–76, but upon receiving reinforcements attacked the British camp near Trois-Rivières on June 8. The attack failed, and the American Army began to retreat toward Lake Champlain. By the end of June, the Americans had withdrawn from Montreal, Fort Chambly, and St. John's. The British halted their pursuit when they reached Lake Champlain, as Carleton wished to build a flotilla to launch an attack toward Crown Point in the south. This delay allowed the American forces to regroup and fortify the southern areas of Lake Champlain.

On October 11, Carleton sailed with his flotilla and captured Crown Point. His force then moved toward Fort Ticonderoga, where the American garrison refused to surrender. With winter coming on, Carleton decided that a blockade of Ticonderoga was not feasible; wintering in that region without adequate shelter would cause casualties, so he withdrew to winter quarters on the frontier of Canada. The Americans had been driven from Canada, but the objectives of the campaign had not been achieved. Fort Ticonderoga and the southern area of Lake

Champlain were still in American hands. As a result, Carleton was branded as being too hesitant, and when the campaign resumed in 1777, the invasion force was under the command of General Burgoyne, who had to finish the job of clearing the southern areas of Lake Champlain.

Southern campaign

A combined force was organized for British operations in the American south. One contingent, under the command of Major- (later Lieutenant-) General Sir Henry Clinton, originated in Boston, while a second was organized to sail from Ireland. Their objectives were to coordinate the raising and support of loyalist corps in the southern colonies. Both contingents encountered problems in reaching their destinations; Clinton arrived at Cape Fear on March 12, after the loyalists of North Carolina had been embodied and soundly defeated at Moore's Creek Bridge on February 27, 1776. Following the arrival of the second contingent, Clinton decided to set sail for South Carolina and capture Sullivan's Island, which protected the estuary leading to Charleston.

The attack on the island highlighted the problems of coordinating an amphibious operation. The naval commander, Admiral Sir Peter Parker, and Clinton communicated poorly, failing to coordinate plans and intelligence. The fort protecting the island, commanded by Colonel William Moultrie, was well fortified, with capable gunners manning the defenses. The British attack began on June 28. The fort not only withstood the attack, but also inflicted heavy damage on the Royal Navy ships. Commanders on land could not launch their attack because the Royal Navy could not get close enough to provide support. The British withdrew and the force sailed for New York to link up with Howe's troops, arriving on August 2.

Middle Atlantic campaign

General Washington sent Major-General Charles Lee, a former British regular, to assess the defenses of the New York City region. Lee understood that defending the region would be too problematic, as the British would certainly have a numerical as well as a naval advantage, permitting them to land troops at will. General Lee decided to fortify areas where the Americans might at least hold up the British regulars and inflict heavy casualties. He was then directed to head south to shore up defenses in South Carolina.

In April, General Washington moved to New York to make preparations for the defense of the region with the remainder of the New England Army. Forts were constructed along the Hudson and designated Forts Lee and Washington. Washington also needed men to defend the area, and summoned some 20,000 soldiers, many of them militia, from the colonies around New York. As Colonel Tallmadge noted: "The American Army [was] composed principally of levies, or troops raised for short periods, and militia" (Tallmadge, p. 8). Washington sent most of his troops to Long Island and constructed fortifications along the heights of Brooklyn and the hills south of the heights. The troops on Long Island were placed under the command of Major-General Israel Putnam, whose defensive lines were poorly organized—too long and too lightly held. Washington, however, approved the plans, and they proceeded accordingly.

Unlike South Carolina, the amphibious operations carried out in New York Harbor were an excellent example of coordinated army/navy planning. Howe and his troops reached New York from Halifax in late June. On July 2, light infantry units seized control of Staten Island. The rest of the British Army was disembarked to camp there for the remainder of July, while Howe awaited reinforcements from Europe and Clinton in the south. The bulk of the reinforcements arrived from Europe in early August, mainly Guards regiments and German auxiliaries.

On August 22, the first British units landed on Long Island. The British officer Kemble wrote: "Landed about 9 in the morning . . . without the smallest opposition . . . the whole on the shore by 12 o'clock making fourteen thousand seven hundred men" (Kemble, p. 85). A force of light infantry, grenadiers, and other regiments proceeded east to reconnoiter the American fortified positions in the hills south of Brooklyn Heights. The British commanders realized that a direct assault would be difficult, while forward units under the command of General Clinton noted that the American left flank was weakly defended. The British decided on a flanking attack to roll the Americans up from behind.

By August 25, all of the British troops, nearly 20,000 men, had been assembled on Long Island. The Battle of Long Island was to be the largest battle of the war in terms of total numbers of men involved. General Howe sent a large force, commanded by General Clinton, to attack the American left flank. Two brigades, under the command of Major-General James Grant, were under orders to attack the American right flank while Clinton's units dealt with the left, creating a diversion. The Hessian Division, under the command of Lieutenant-General Leopold von Heister, was to attack the American center, commanded by Major-General John Sullivan.

Clinton's force moved into position overnight on August 26–27, and General Grant's brigades began to move toward the American lines. A British captain described how "we got through the pass at daybreak without any opposition . . . we fired two pieces of cannon to let him [General Grant] know we were at hand" (Scheer and Rankin, p. 166). The battle began at 9:00 AM with General Grant's troops and the Hessian division attacking.

The American Colonel Tallmadge commented, "Before such an overwhelming force of disciplined troops, our small band could not maintain their ground, and the main body retired within their lines" (Tallmadge, p. 9). The British and Hessians smashed into the American center, which began to collapse. The fighting in the trenches and redoubts was quite bloody. A British officer described how "the Hessians and our brave Highlanders gave no quarter, and it was a fine sight to see with what alacrity they dispatched

the Rebels with their bayonets after we surrounded them" (Scheer and Rankin, p. 167).

The American right flank held up better than the center line until Clinton's force began to attack from the rear. Some of the fiercest fighting took place as the American right flank attempted to pull back. The troops of the Maryland regiments acquitted themselves well in attempting to force a hole in the British lines. After a series of heavy fights in the marshes behind their positions, the American right wing broke up into small parties and attempted to reach the fortified lines at Brooklyn Heights.

Colonel Tallmadge recorded the bitterness of the fighting on Long Island: "This was the first time in my life that I had witnessed the awful scene of a battle . . . I well remember my sensations on the occasion, for they were solemn beyond description" (Tallmadge, pp. 9–10). An American private soldier recalled how, when his unit was shipped over to Long Island to support the defenses at Brooklyn Heights, "[They] now began to meet the wounded men, another sight I was unacquainted with, some with broken arms, some with broken legs, and some with broken heads" (Martin, p. 24).

Battle of Long Island. (Colonial Williamsburg)

The British were outside the defenses of Brooklyn Heights by midday, but Howe decided not to attack right away. He feared that the defenses were too strong, although he was mistaken in this assumption and they might have been easily breached. By 10:00 PM on August 29, the Americans had begun to withdraw 9,000 men from Long Island and retreat to Manhattan, over the East River. The British were not aware of the withdrawal and as one British officer noted: "In the morning, to our great astonishment, found they had evacuated all their works on Brookland [Brooklyn]" (Kemble, p. 86). Part of the reason for this was, as pointed out by Colonel Tallmadge, that "the troops began to retire from the lines in such a manner that no chasm was made in the lines" (Tallmadge, p. 10). It is estimated that the Americans lost nearly 3,000 men killed and wounded, plus another 1,500 captured. The British lost 300 men killed and 500 wounded.

General Howe did not move against Washington's army on Manhattan Island because peace negotiations were still a possibility. The Declaration of Independence proved a stumbling block, however, and on September 15, 4,000 British troops landed on Manhattan Island at Kip's Bay, after clearing most of the western end of Long Island. The British decided to secure the beachhead area instead of attempting to cut off the retreating American forces from lower Manhattan. This strategy allowed the Americans to retreat up the west side of Manhattan Island.

A combined force of Hessians and British light infantry was repulsed at Harlem Heights in northern Manhattan on September 16. The Americans held fortified positions at the northern end of the island, and the British decided not to attack frontally. Instead, they embarked and landed to the north of Manhattan on October 12. Washington recognized the danger of being cut off, and decided to pull most of his troops off the island and into Westchester County of New York, leaving a large contingent at Fort Washington while the

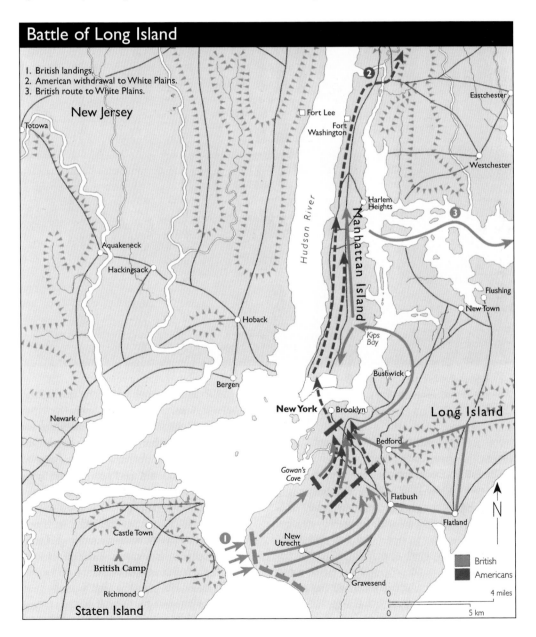

Battle of Long Island

1. British landings.
2. American withdrawal to White Plains.
3. British route to White Plains.

New Jersey

Totowa

Fort Lee

Fort Washington

Eastchester

Westchester

Aquakeneck

Hackingsack

Hudson River

Harlem Heights

Manhattan Island

Flushing

New Town

Hoback

Kips Bay

Bushwick

Bergen

Newark

New York   Brooklyn

Long Island

Bedford

Gowan's Cove

Flatbush

Flatland

N

Castle Town

New Utrecht

British Camp

Gravesend

British

Americans

Richmond

Staten Island

0   4 miles

0   5 km

British troops enter New York City.
(The British Museum)

majority withdrew to White Plains and entrenched themselves there.

The British forces attacked the American positions at White Plains on October 28. Colonel Tallmadge reported that "at dawn of the day, the Hessian column advanced within musket shot of our troops . . . at first they fell back, but rallyed [rallied] again immediately" (Tallmadge, p. 14). The focus of the battle was Chadderton's Hill, which dominated the area and was held by the Americans. After two attempts, British forces took the hill, and the

rest of the day was spent with the two sides exchanging cannon and small-arms fire. After a few days, General Washington withdrew further afield with his troops. Here again, General Howe failed to press his advantage to try to capture and destroy Washington's army. Instead he returned to Manhattan Island to besiege Fort Washington.

The British Lieutenant-General Earl Hugh Percy had previously made an attempt on Fort Washington from the south but had recognized that it was well defended. By November 15, the fort was surrounded on all sides by British troops, including Royal Navy ships on the Hudson River. George

November 20. Cornwallis was able to threaten Fort Lee, which was evacuated. He pushed hard to entrap Washington and his army. Howe followed and landed with another contingent, meeting up with Cornwallis at New Brunswick, New Jersey, in early December. Howe also dispatched a contingent of 7,000 men under the command of General Clinton to seize Newport, Rhode Island. Both the town and the island on which it was located were in British hands by December 8, giving the British control of Narragansett Bay.

Cornwallis and Howe together chased Washington and his army across New Jersey. On December 8, Washington and his army crossed the Delaware River as the British entered Trenton. On December 14, the British were ordered into winter quarters in New Jersey. British and Hessian troops were quartered throughout the region, and General Washington devised a bold scheme. He decided to attack the Hessian positions in Trenton on December 25, and his plan was completely successful. The Hessians were soundly defeated, for two reasons: the Hessian Colonel Rall had failed to fortify their positions; and the date of the attack meant that many soldiers had been celebrating the holiday. The Americans lost four men wounded, compared with more than 1,000 Hessians captured.

Washington re-crossed the Delaware on the night of December 25, only to go back again on December 27, when he headed toward Trenton. Howe had ordered Cornwallis and 8,000 troops to find and destroy Washington's force. Cornwallis' force came into contact with Washington in Trenton on January 2, 1777. A Hessian officer noted: "The jägers and light infantry, supported by the Hessian Grenadiers, attacked the enemy at once, whereupon he withdrew through Trenton across the bridge" (Ewald, p. 49). Washington was caught at Assunpink Creek. During the evening, however, Washington, realizing his position, marched first due east then due north toward Princeton. Ewald described "this clever man [Washington] who did not doubt

Washington withdrew across the Hudson into New Jersey on November 16, but a large group of troops remained stationed on the eastern side of the river, under the command of General Lee, to forestall any British incursion into southern New England.

On November 16, Fort Washington was attacked from three sides. The fort fell with more than 3,000 American soldiers killed, wounded, or captured, and American control of the Hudson was compromised. Following this victory, Howe decided to divide his forces. He sent Major- (later Lieutenant-) General Earl Charles Cornwallis and 4,000 soldiers to Closter, New Jersey, on that Lord Cornwallis would realize his mistake during the night and would dispatch a corps ... whereby he would be forced by circumstances to surrender" (Ewald, p. 49).

The British forces at Princeton were surprised and compelled to give ground. Washington, however, was forced to head to the mountains in Morristown when news arrived that Cornwallis was heading toward Princeton. Morristown offered Washington the option of counteracting a British move from either New York to the north along the Hudson or across New Jersey toward Philadelphia.

The British had lost more than 1,000 men in the course of one week. Howe pulled his forces back to New Brunswick, thus abandoning most of New Jersey. As with operations in Canada, the British were put on the defensive and would have to regain lost ground in the campaigns of 1777, when they aimed to seize Philadelphia. The successes of late 1776 had given the American cause a significant boost in morale. An American soldier commented that "our taking the Hessians has given our affairs quite a different turn as the militia are embodying in all parts of the Jerseys" (Shaw Papers Ms. N-49.47). The Hessian officer, Ewald, appraised public opinion of Washington and Cornwallis:

[Actions at Trenton and Princeton] raised so much hubbub and sensation in the world and gave Washington the reputation of an excellent general, derived simply and solely from Lord Cornwallis' mistake of not marching in two columns to Trenton (Ewald, p. 50).

The British had lost the initiative and were clearly no longer within striking distance of Philadelphia, the perceived governmental headquarters of the Thirteen Colonies. George Washington and the remnants of his army had survived the 1776 campaigns. The foundations of the Continental Army had been laid. A French officer writing a report described the American forces thus: "Men need only the experience of defeats in order

to learn how to defend themselves properly and acquire the military effectiveness necessary in order to inspire respect on the enemy" (Recicourt, p. 211).

The land war: 1777

The British strategy for 1777 provides the clearest example of poor strategic planning by generals in North America. General Burgoyne and his army were ordered to push south from Canada and take Albany and the Hudson River. Burgoyne was expected to wait in Albany to link up with General Howe. General Howe did not see that

Burgoyne required his support, and, holed up in New York with his troops, decided that they would not link up with Burgoyne as planned. Leaving only a secondary group in New York to push north, Howe took the major part of the British army in New York and set out to seize Philadelphia by amphibious assault. Howe felt that, since Philadelphia represented the independence movement, the seizure of the Continental Congress might force an end to the conflict.

Historians have debated the "what ifs" of this decision-making process thoroughly, but it is indisputably clear that both Howe and Burgoyne underestimated the American forces and paid a high price for their miscalculation. The war became global partly due to the incompetent performance of 1777. After the campaigns of 1777, Great Britain would be forced to strip her army in North America to fight a global war against France and later Spain and the Dutch Republic.

The "Main" Continental Army, under the command of General Washington, was deployed to counter the British attacks in Pennsylvania. It suffered defeats in this undertaking but survived, never being completely destroyed. The "Separate Army,"

British amphibious attack on Newport, Rhode Island. (National Maritime Museum)

now referred to as the "Northern Army," under the command of General Philip Schuyler with Major-General Horatio Gates as his subordinate, formed to fight Burgoyne's army. The majority of troops used to defend New York from the British were made up of militia from New England and New York, with Continentals representing a small corps of the total numbers.

Northern campaign

The principal northern campaign began in Canada. Lieutenant-General Burgoyne advanced from St. John's, Quebec, toward Lake Champlain with 10,000 men in June 1777. A secondary drive of 1,600 troops, regulars, provincials, and Indians was sent from Fort Oswego in the west under the command of Lieutenant-Colonel Barry St. Leger. St. Leger was to march due east along the Mohawk River and link up with Burgoyne at Albany.

Burgoyne's force reached Fort Ticonderoga on July 1. The American commander at Ticonderoga, Brigadier Arthur St. Clair, expected the attack to come from the front, but General Burgoyne placed cannon on a hill opposite. St. Clair, recognizing the danger, withdrew his force of 3,000 militia and Continentals to the south on July 5. Leaving a small detachment at Ticonderoga to maintain communications with Canada, Burgoyne pushed south to harass St. Clair's rearguards, reaching Skenesboro by July 10.

At Skenesboro, Burgoyne decided to march overland to Forts Ann and Edward instead of returning north to travel down Lake George. The Americans anticipated Burgoyne's plan, and set out to block his path. A British officer, Lieutenant William Digby, noted on July 24:

The enemy have felled large trees over the roads which were turned so narrow as not to allow more than one man ... we were obliged to cut around the wood which was attended by much fatigue and labour (Add. Mss. 32413).

Supplies became a problem early in the campaign; Burgoyne commented on July 9

and 10, "the army much fatigued, many parts of it having wanted their provisions for two days" (7204-6-4). He also described the effect of the terrain: "The toil of the march was great ... forty bridges to construct and others to repair" (7204-6-4).

The British reached Fort Edward on the Hudson River on July 30, and occupied Fort George on the same day. The Americans were still falling back to the south and across the river in the Saratoga region, but the ever-present need for supplies forced the British to stop and rest at Fort Edward. On August 11, a detachment of 600 men, comprising German auxiliaries, provincial troops, and Indians, under the command of Lieutenant-Colonel Frederick Baum, was instructed to march southeast toward Bennington, "to obtain large supplies of cattle, horses, and carriages" (7204-6-4). Brigadier John Stark and 2,000 New England militiamen met Baum's column outside Bennington on August 16, where they surrounded and destroyed them. A second German column, which had been sent in aid of Baum's efforts on August 14, closed in on Bennington as the militia pillaged Baum's camp. The militia re-formed to destroy the second column as well. Burgoyne shortly received word of the defeat and loss of almost 1,000 men.

Lieutenant Digby wrote on August 20 that "the German detachment at Bennington was destroyed and ... St. Leger was forced to retire to Oswego" (Add. Mss. 32413). On August 19, Major-General Gates took over command of the Northern Army from General Schuyler. Recruits were on the rise as word of the successes at Bennington spread and raised spirits in the area. On September 13–14, Burgoyne's army crossed the Hudson River near Saratoga. Supplies were still at a premium for the British, and an officer in the Royal Artillery described a general order that warned troops to "be cautious of expending their ammunition in case of action ... the impossibility of a fresh supply ... avoid firing on a retreating army" (Hadden, p. 150).

Upon taking command, General Gates marched north toward Bemis Heights, which controlled the main Saratoga–Albany road. General Schuyler had fortified Bemis Heights in August. The first firefight between the two armies occurred on September 18, when British soldiers foraging for food were ambushed by American forces. On September 19, Burgoyne set out to deal with Bemis Heights, only to be intercepted by Major-General Benedict Arnold, who smashed into the British column with 3,000 troops at Freeman's Farm. The fighting was heavy; Lieutenant Digby related that "the clash of cannon and musketry never ceased till darkness ... when they [Americans] retired to their camp leaving us the master of the field, but it was a dear bought victory" (Add. Mss. 32413). The British suffered more than 600 men killed and wounded in this incident, while the Americans lost just over 300 men killed and wounded. Burgoyne decided to stay in the area and build a defensive position for the army after he received word from

Lieutenant-General Clinton in New York, promising a push up the Hudson River.

Clinton marched north with 3,000 troops on October 3, and his force moved quickly, seizing Verplanck's Point, as well as Forts Montgomery, Constitution, and Clinton by October 7. Clinton sent a detachment of 2,000 men and supplies toward Albany to meet Burgoyne, whose situation was rapidly deteriorating. The Americans had all but cut off communications between Burgoyne and Canada, seized Fort George, and threatened Fort Ticonderoga.

Burgoyne decided to attack the American positions at Bemis Heights once again on October 7, instead of falling back toward the Hudson. He sent a strong force to engage the American left flank; this was repulsed and fell back to the British lines. An American soldier noted, "A body of the enemy [was] advancing toward our lines ... at about 4 o'clock the

Shooting of British Brigadier Simon Fraser by American Sharpshooters, October 7, 1777. (National Archives of Canada)

Northern campaigns

CANADA

Quebec

St Lawrence

Trois Rivieres

Ottawa

Montreal

St Lawrence

Lake
Champlain

MASSACHUSETTS
(MAINE)

Lake
Ontario

Oswego

Fort Stanwix

Mohawk

Fort Dayton

Fort Ticonderoga
Hubbardton
Fort Anne
Fort George
Fort Edward
Saratoga
Bemis Heights
Albany

Bennington

NEW HAMPSHIRE

Connecticut

Portsmouth

NEW YORK

Boston

MASSACHUSETTS

Hudson

Delaware

West Point   Fort
Constitution

Forts Clinton
& Montgomery

CONNECTICUT

RHODE
ISLAND

Newport

PENNSYLVANIA

NEW
JERSEY

New York

Susquehanna

Trenton

| | 0 | | 50 miles |
| | 0 | | 100 km |

Campaigns of Carleton, 1776
Campaigns of Burgoyne, St Leger and Clinton, 1777
Campaigns of Montgomery and Arnold, 1775
■ American fort

battle began ... the rifles and light infantry fell upon the enemy's right flank and rear ... they then retreated with great precipitation and confusion" (Dearborn, p. 108). British morale was very low, and sank further when Clinton's detachment was forced to return after the pilots refused to proceed any further up the Hudson, leaving Burgoyne's troops stranded and outnumbered two to one.

On October 8, Burgoyne decided to pull back, only to discover that Gates had already cut off his retreat. Burgoyne created a defended camp north of Saratoga and the Americans began to close in. Lieutenant Digby observed: "Their cannon and ours began to play on each other. They took many of our batteaus [boats] on the river as our artillery could not protect them" (Add.

Mss. 32413). Another British officer noted: "We are now become so habituated to fire that the soldiers seem to be indifferent to it" (Anburey, p. 181).

On October 14, Burgoyne began to negotiate the surrender of his forces, and on October 17 the remains of his force marched out of camp. The British surrendered almost 6,000 men, shattering British prestige the world over. The surrender effectively removed any threat to the Hudson River region and New England from the north. The American forces had distinguished themselves, but the British commanders had forgotten the rules they had learned in the French-Indian War about waging war in the hilly, wooded countryside of the American frontier. The American generals, especially Arnold, had demonstrated themselves equal to the task required of them. The militia had fought well when they had the advantage of terrain, as at Bennington, while the Continentals had fought well at Freeman's Farm.

Middle Atlantic campaign

Howe's campaign in the Middle Atlantic centered around the engagements at Brandywine and Germantown. He moved troops into New Jersey in an attempt to draw Washington and the "Main Army" out for battle. This maneuver produced a series of skirmishes, but was a failure overall, prompting Howe to return to Staten Island. Over the course of July, troops embarked onto Royal Navy ships and transports, and on July 23 the fleet sailed. On August 25, the fleet landed its cargo on the northern reaches of Chesapeake Bay at the Head of Elk. Washington received word of the landing and marched south with the Main Army, 18,000 strong, to confront the British (Tallmadge, p. 20). Washington placed his army at Brandywine Creek and built up the area into a defensive position.

Though strong generally, the American position had left its flanks unprotected. Howe, approaching with his troops, realized

The Carribbean

the potential for another successful flank attack. An American soldier described how, "at 8 o'clock in the morning on the 11th [September] a considerable body of the enemy appeared opposite to us" (Shaw Ms. N-49.47).

The battle commenced at 10:00 AM. A sizeable column of Hessian and British units were sent in opposite the center and left flank of the American lines, under the command of Lieutenant-General Wilhelm von Knyphausen. A large formation of light infantry, plus Guards and Grenadiers units, under the command of General Cornwallis, moved without being detected against the American right flank, in a march 18 miles (30 km) long, intending to create havoc in the American lines. The other British lines were successful in pushing the American lines back, and the British left flank finally joined the battle at about 4:00 PM. As Major John Andre noted: "The rebels were driven back by the superior fire of the troops, but these troops were too much exhausted to be able to charge or pursue" (Andre, p. 46).

The Americans reacted but did not panic. When the British left flank finally smashed through the American lines, the Americans began to retreat, but in fairly good order, not as a rabble. A French officer serving with the American forces declared: "If the English had followed up their advantages that day, Washington's Army would have been spoken of no more" (5701-9).

The battle at Brandywine Creek cost the Americans more than 1,000 men killed, wounded, and captured. The British lost half that number. The British had won but were not in a position to follow up their victory aggressively; they were simply too tired after marching 18 miles (30 km). The two armies fell back toward Philadelphia over the next few weeks and a series of small skirmishes took place. On September 26, the British marched into Philadelphia. This was an important achievement psychologically, but not as important strategically as Howe's continued failure to completely destroy Washington's Main Army as it withdrew to the west of the city. The Continental Congress had already been evacuated to Lancaster and later moved to Yorktown. Howe moved to the north of the city and encamped his army at Germantown.

Following the defeat and occupation of Philadelphia, Washington set out to destroy the British camp at Germantown. He deployed four columns, two militia and two Continental, intended to converge on the

Battle of Germantown. (Anne SK Brown Collection)

British lines simultaneously. An American private soldier recorded that at:

About daybreak [October 4] our advanced guard and the British outposts came in contact ... they soon fell back and we advanced, when the action became general. The enemy [was] driven quite through their camp. They left their kettles ... affairs went on well for some time (Martin, pp. 72–73).

The American advance became bogged down in trying to take a position held by the 40th Regiment at Chew House. As Major Andre noted, "These [soldiers of the 40th Regiment] not only maintained themselves a great while but drove the rebels off repeatedly" (Andre, p. 55). By the time the Americans moved on, the rest of the British forces had rallied. Colonel Tallmadge stated, "During this transaction [Chew House] time elapsed, the situation of our troops was uncomfortable, their ardor abated, and the enemy obtained time to rally. In less than thirty minutes, our troops began to retire, and from the ardor of the pursuit, were in full retreat" (Tallmadge, pp. 22–23).

Not all of Washington's troops took part in the battle due to the weather, but again the British were unable to follow up their victory to encircle and destroy the Main Army. The losses for the Americans were some 1,000 killed, wounded, and captured, while the British lost 500 men.

Howe pulled back his defensive lines around the city of Philadelphia, and once again the British found themselves on the defensive with the Americans, although weakened, still able to inflict damage upon their troops. The British cleared defenses on the Delaware River to allow seaborne supplies to reach the city. Washington was having difficulty keeping his army together, as enlistment contracts expired for many men. This depletion convinced Washington not to attack, but Howe was left once again at the end of 1777 without a decisive victory to his credit. Washington withdrew his army into winter quarters at Valley Forge, Pennsylvania, in mid-December, where the troops were retrained under the drill instructor eyes of Major-General von Steuben.

The campaign of 1777 finally ended in November. The British had been soundly defeated at Saratoga, and the war seemed likely to become a global conflict with the entrance of France. Howe had defeated the Main Army, but had been unable to conclusively destroy it. The American "capitol" had been taken, but even this decisive action did not signify the end of the war. The year 1778 marked the true beginning of the end of the British presence in the Thirteen Colonies. Both the British Army and the Royal Navy were redirected to other parts of the world to deal with French and, later, Spanish antagonism. The years 1775–77, in retrospect, were the closest the British came to ending the uprising with military force. It is debatable whether the political rebellion would have continued if the American forces had been decisively defeated in a land war.

The land war: 1778

The British forces in North America were centered around New York, Philadelphia, Newport, Florida, Halifax, Quebec, and Montreal. A formal alliance, signed on February 6, 1778, between the American and French governments, forced a change of strategy. Over the first few months of the year, Benjamin Franklin was instrumental in lobbying the French court to support the American cause. British commanders were reassigned. General Clinton was ordered to take command of the forces in the Thirteen Colonies, replacing General Howe. In Canada, General Carleton was replaced by Lieutenant-General Frederick Haldimand.

Senior commanders in North America and Great Britain realized that the focus of war had shifted fundamentally, and that France had become the primary threat. In March, Clinton received his orders for the whole of 1778. He was to withdraw British forces from Philadelphia, and send troops to New York and then to the West Indies to fight the French. The British were to hold New York, Newport, and Canada. Naval raids were scheduled along the New England coast, and a southern campaign was planned. The overarching strategy was that the British Army would control major towns along the coast, and the navy would allow it to raid at will. Peace negotiations were to be opened between the Continental Congress and the British government.

Middle Atlantic campaign

General Washington and his Main Army had a difficult winter at Valley Forge, 18 miles (30 km) north of Philadelphia. Many men were released from duty when their enlistment contracts expired, but a corps of men and officers remained who were properly trained for linear warfare, thanks to the training program created by Major-General von Steuben and battle experience gained. Colonel Tallmadge noted on the eve of the 1778 campaign that the Main Army began "feeling somewhat like veteran troops" (Tallmadge, p. 27).Washington used the winter to develop a plan for militia to be used to guard specific areas, releasing Continental troops and extra militia units for mobile operations. In spite of this, personnel shortfalls continued. The number of men enlisted was still well below the army's authorized strengths, which limited Washington's ability to attack Philadelphia. Many historians consider the Continental Army that marched out of Valley Forge against Clinton's army the most highly trained and disciplined American force of the entire conflict.

On May 8, General Clinton arrived in Philadelphia to take over command from General Howe. Clinton was ordered to withdraw from Philadelphia, and decided to march overland to Sandy Hook, New Jersey. Three thousand loyalists who feared for their safety were shipped by sea to New York, and, on June 18, Clinton set off with nearly 10,000 troops and more loyalist refugees toward New York. An American soldier remembered: "We heard the British army had left Philadelphia ... we marched immediately in pursuit" (Martin, p. 122). The American force shadowed the withdrawing British Army, monitoring the train of supplies and men, which stretched for 12 miles (19 km). Very high temperatures made for very slow going.

Major-General Charles Lee was sent with 5,000 men to harass the British rearguard, while the rest of the Main Army stayed further back. On June 28, Washington ordered Lee to attack the rearguards, although he was not certain of their size. Lee sent in the attack near Monmouth Court House. The fighting quickly became confused; as British officer Kemble noted: "Lee then advanced to begin the attack, but falling in with our two Grenadiers Battalions, and a Battalion of Guards, who facing about charged and pushed them above two miles [3.2 km]" (Kemble, p. 154). This account was confirmed by an American soldier: "Our division under the command of General Lee advanced toward the enemy. They formed in a solid column, then fired a volley at us; they being so much superior to our numbers, we retreated" (Greenman, p. 122).

Lee had smashed into the British Second Division, led by General Cornwallis. Washington deployed the remainder of his army to face the British counterattack, the brunt of which was borne by New England regiments. A heated verbal exchange occurred between Lee and Washington following Lee's retreat. Lee was relieved of command and would later face court martial for not obeying orders. Lee was also suspected of being a British sympathizer. An American soldier, describing the scene, said: "A sharp conflict ensued; these troops [New Englanders] maintained their ground until the whole force of the enemy that could be brought to bear had charged upon them" (Scheer and Rankin, p. 331). Major Andre described how "this column [American] appeared to our left and rear, marching very rapidly and in good order" (Andre, pp. 78–79). The British, while successful at points along the line, launched attacks without proper orders and were unable to maintain consistent pressure.

Lieutenant General Sir Henry Clinton.
(Anne SK Brown Collection)

The battle was the longest of the war, beginning in early morning and lasting all day. Small pieces of land were exchanged, as were artillery duels. General Washington was able to push the British back to their original positions by the early evening. The American forces succeeded in holding the line against a British assault in the open field and retaking lost territory. The heat of the day had taken a toll, however, and neither side attempted another assault as night approached. Clinton withdrew his force when evening fell, unmolested by the Americans. He was running short of supplies, and needed to reach Sandy Hook and meet the Royal Navy. The British had lost nearly 1,000 men killed, wounded, and captured, while the American forces had lost just half that.

The outcome of the Battle of Monmouth was indecisive. The Americans claimed victory, but Clinton disputed "the manifest misapplication of that term [victory] to an army whose principle is retreat and which accomplishes it without affront or loss" (Clinton, p. 97). Clinton was able to withdraw to Sandy Hook and was evacuated to New York by July 6, before the French fleet arrived, so he had fulfilled his orders. The British had failed to destroy or even force the Americans from the battlefield, which provided another morale boost for the Americans. More important, the Americans successfully counter-attacked and seized ground in the open. As a Hessian officer commented:

Today the Americans showed much boldness and resolution on all sides during their attacks. Had Generals Washington and Lee not attacked so early, but waited longer, until our army had pushed deeper into the very difficult defiles in this area, it is quite possible we would have been routed (Ewald, p. 136).

Northern campaign

On July 11, a French fleet, carrying 4,000 soldiers, arrived off Sandy Hook under the command of Admiral Charles Hector Comte d'Estaing. Clinton's successful withdrawal and redeployment meant that New York was no longer a feasible target, and the fleet shortly sailed for Newport, Rhode Island, arriving off the coast on July 29. On August 9, a second force, this one American and commanded by Major-General John Sullivan, arrived with 10,000 Continental and militia troops, to invest the British position from the north. The British had 3,000 troops at Newport under the command of General Sir Robert Pigot.

The French fleet was followed closely by British Admiral Lord Howe, who arrived off the coast in August to lift the siege. Evaluating the opposition, Major John Bowater noted: "The French fleet is heavier than ours, but we outnumber them" (Balderston and Syrett, p. 167). The French fleet set out to engage the British, only to run into a storm on August 11 that damaged both. The weather forced the French to withdraw to Boston, which in turn caused problems for the American land forces, as the British continued to be resupplied, reinforced, and supported by the Royal Navy.

General Sullivan was irate with d'Estaing's withdrawal, which forced the Americans to lift the siege by August 27. This episode soured relations between the French and American commanders, as each side accused the other of lack of effort. A British relieving force under the command of Major-General Charles Grey arrived at Newport after the French withdrawal. Supported by the Royal Navy, a series of raids began along the New England coast, destroying supplies and ships and gathering stores from remote places such as Martha's Vineyard.

Coastal raiding was not all; during the summer and autumn months, a series of raids led by British provincial corps, including Butler's Rangers and allied Indian tribes, struck from Fort Niagara along the frontiers of New York and Virginia. Fighting along the frontier had been increasing steadily throughout 1778, and raids had struck settlements as far east as Cherry Valley, 50 miles (80 km) west of Albany. American efforts to counterattack were unsuccessful, and by the end of 1778 Washington and his senior officers were drawing up campaign plans for 1779.

Southern campaign

In November, Clinton released 5,000 troops for operations in Florida and the West Indies. Meanwhile, Lieutenant-Colonel Archibald Campbell was sent with 3,000 troops, both regulars and provincials, to seize Savannah, Georgia. The Americans at Savannah, under the command of Major-General Robert Howe, were a small detachment, and were easily defeated on December 29. Savannah fell, as did the surrounding area. Campbell continued northwest, and his force reached and captured Augusta, Georgia, near the end of January 1779.

Outside the Thirteen Colonies

The French were the first to move in the materially important West Indies, seizing the British island of Dominica on September 7, 1778. The British went on the offensive in December; they landed on St. Lucia on

December 13, after reinforcements had arrived from New York, occupying the northern side of the island. Admiral d'Estaing landed 7,000 reinforcements on the opposite end of the island, and on December 18 the French attempted to destroy the British fortifications. Their efforts were unsuccessful and they suffered heavy casualties, forcing them to

withdraw on December 29 and surrender the island to the British force.

The British East India Company was embroiled in a war with the Maratha Confederacy. Word reached Bombay and Madras of the French intervention on the American side, prompting British East India Company forces to move against French posts in India. All of these had been seized by the end of 1778, except for Mahe. In taking this action, however, the British sparked a war (also known as the Second Mysore War) with the local ruler,

Battle of Monmouth Court House.
(The National Army Museum)

Haidar Ali of Mysore, who had been partially allied with the French. The war in India largely pitched the British East India Company and regular forces against the Indian princes' armies until at least 1782, when a strong French force came to the aid of Haidar Ali.

The campaigns of 1778 clearly illustrate the shift of British focus from North America to the colonial interests throughout the world threatened by the French. The Americans took advantage of the situation and proved themselves in battle at Monmouth. The Continental Army continued to have difficulties but remained in good order as it went into winter quarters for 1778–79. The British were hemmed in at New York and Newport, and it was apparent that the focus of the war was going to shift to land campaigns in the south. Monmouth, the longest battle of the war, was also the last major battle in the north. From 1779, the war in northern New York and the southern colonies was to become even more bitter as loyalists, Indians, and rebels fought fiercely for control of the interior.

The land war: 1779

The campaigns of 1779 in North America were relatively small compared to previous years. There were minor operations at Stony Point on the Hudson River and along the Penobscot River in Massachusetts (present-day Maine). There was a successful American campaign against Indian and loyalist raiders on the frontier. The remainder of North American operations occurred in the south. The principal reason for both the smaller-scale battles and geographical shift was that Spain entered the war against Britain in 1779, putting British interests around the world in still greater danger. The British also believed that the colonies in the south might be more loyal to the British cause.

Northern campaign

On June 16, 1779, British Brigadier Francis McLean landed at Castine, Massachusetts, on Penobscot Bay with 600 regulars. The town was strategically located to offset New England privateering efforts against British shipping. A Massachusetts militia force of 1,000 men, under the command of Brigadier Solomon Lovell, was dispatched to remove the British, landing on July 28. The Americans decided to lay siege to the fort instead of undertaking an immediate assault. A Royal Navy force arrived to lift the siege on August 13, compelling the Massachusetts militia to withdraw into the woods and the American ships in the bay to be scuttled.

Washington ordered Major-General Sullivan, along with 2,500 Continentals and militia, to march from Eaton, Pennsylvania, toward Fort Niagara, New York, in May. A second force of 1,500 New York militia, commanded by Brigadier James Clinton, was to meet up with Sullivan and lay waste to the Indian lands from Pennsylvania into New York. Sullivan understood how to operate in the woods, and deployed small units of skirmishers to protect the flanks of his force. John Butler, the commander of the loyalist Butler's Rangers, set out to fortify the local tribes for the onslaught.

The two American forces met on August 22, and set to work burning the harvests and villages of the Indians. On August 27, Butler, with 250 Rangers, joined by 600 Indians commanded by Joseph Brant, prepared to meet the 4,000 Americans. The two forces met at Newtown on August 29–30. The Americans successfully avoided an ambush, and the Indians and Rangers were pushed out. They headed toward Fort Niagara, opening the Genesee and Mohawk valleys to the American forces. The Americans destroyed 40 villages and nearly 160,000 bushels of corn. The Indian population flooded toward Fort Niagara. The operation was successful for the Americans, but it did not signal the end of the raids along the frontier. Joseph Brant, along with his Indian warriors and Butler's Rangers, would return.

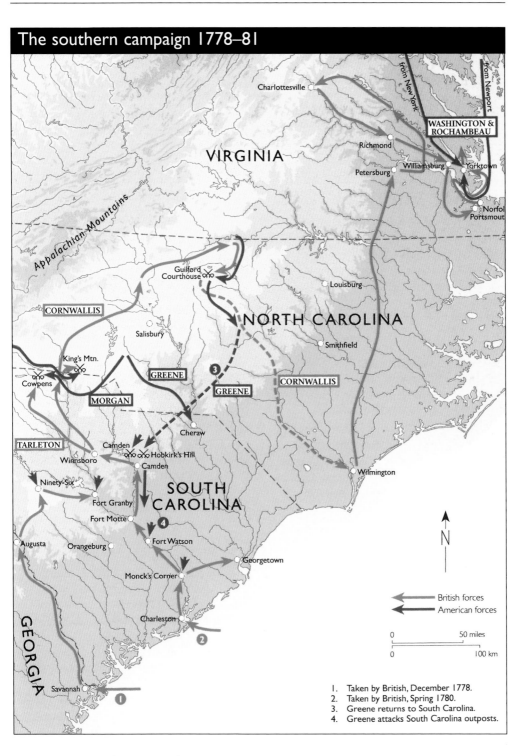

The southern campaign 1778–81

- Charlottesville
- *from New York*
- *from Newport*
- Richmond
- **WASHINGTON & ROCHAMBEAU**
- VIRGINIA
- Williamsburg
- Yorktown
- Petersburg
- Norfol
- Portsmout
- *Appalachian Mountains*
- Guilford Courthouse
- Louisburg
- **CORNWALLIS**
- NORTH CAROLINA
- Salisbury
- Smithfield
- King's Mtn.
- Cowpens
- **GREENE**
- ❸
- **CORNWALLIS**
- **GREENE**
- **MORGAN**
- Cheraw
- **TARLETON**
- Camden
- Hobkirk's Hill
- Winnsboro
- Camden
- Ninety-Six
- SOUTH CAROLINA
- Fort Granby
- Fort Motte
- ❹
- Augusta
- Orangeburg
- Fort Watson
- Monck's Corner
- Georgetown
- Wilmington
- N
- Charleston
- ❷
- GEORGIA
- Savannah
- ❶

British forces
American forces

| 0 | | 50 miles |
| 0 | | 100 km |

1. Taken by British, December 1778.
2. Taken by British, Spring 1780.
3. Greene returns to South Carolina.
4. Greene attacks South Carolina outposts.

Middle Atlantic campaign

Clinton advanced north from New York in late May, and seized Stony Point and Verplanck's Point on the Hudson River on June 1. He hoped by this action to force Washington to leave the defended regions of West Point and seek battle in the open, but Washington did not fall into his trap.

Clinton next arranged for a series of raids along the Connecticut coast, trying to make Washington move east into New England. Washington not only failed to take the bait, but retook Stony Point on July 15 instead. As Colonel Tallmadge noted, "Such was the ardour and impetuosity of the Americans, that they surmounted all difficulties ... and captured the whole garrison in a short time with bayonet alone" (Tallmadge, p. 31).

Verplanck's Point remained in British hands. The British recalled all troops from the Connecticut coastal raids and moved toward Stony Point. The Americans withdrew, destroying defenses as they went. From this point, the fighting in the Hudson River and New York City areas deteriorated into an ongoing series of skirmishes between units foraging and undertaking reconnaissance.

Southern campaign

Lieutenant-Colonel Campbell had succeeded in taking Savannah and Augusta in 1778, but not all of Georgia had been subdued. Brigadier-General Augustine Prevost arrived in late January 1779 with a second British contingent from Florida, also taking over as the senior British commander. Major-General Benjamin Lincoln, meanwhile, replaced General Howe as commander of the American forces in the south.

The British abandoned Augusta in March, following reports of a large Carolina militia marching south, leaving loyalists in the interior exposed to pro-independence factions. Brigadier Prevost marched to Charleston, South Carolina, and laid siege to the town. Lincoln received news of Prevost's move and turned toward Charleston in pursuit. Prevost was outnumbered, and was forced to lift the siege on May 12. Lincoln followed Prevost's force as it withdrew, and the two forces skirmished at Stono Ferry in late June. Prevost then moved his troops back toward Georgia, while the Americans requested support from the French Admiral d'Estaing.

D'Estaing arrived off Savannah on September 1 with 3,500 French troops, who landed on September 12, as Lincoln and his force were moving in from the north. Prevost was able to delay the impending French attack by asking for a few days to decide whether to surrender, although in fact he was using this time to wait for reinforcements to arrive to strengthen the defenses. By October 5, the French siege batteries were in place and American forces ringed the town. A French officer noted on October 6 that this course of action was a mistake: "We should not have constructed works. In doing so, we afforded the English time to strengthen theirs. We regret that we did not attack on the first day" (Jones, p. 26).

The French command was anxious to end the siege, and on October 9 the combined French and American forces attacked. Prevost had foreknowledge of the attack from a deserter in his camp. The attack began in the early hours of the morning, described by a French officer as "a very lively fire of musketry and of cannon upon our troops from the trenches" (Jones, p. 30). Men from the South Carolina Continentals and French forces were able to seize a few ramparts, but were ultimately forced back with "disorder in the columns" (Jones, p. 36). The American and French forces lacked a coordinated attack plan, and within three hours the attack was called off.

The British forces lost 16 men, and the Americans and French more than 1,000 killed and wounded (Jones, p. 37). On October 18, d'Estaing left, taking the French fleet with him. Lincoln, as Sullivan in Newport had been before him, was angered by this decision. So far, American–French cooperation had not proved a decisive factor in the North American campaign.

The British decided to stage a combined naval/land raid to relieve pressure on Prevost and the British regulars and loyalists in Georgia. On May 5, 1779, a fleet of 1,800 men departed from New York, landing at Hampton Roads, Virginia on May 11. The army set out to destroy all the tobacco stockpiles and shipping in the area. The

Major General Charles Lee. (Anne SK Brown Collection)

ABOVE Siege of Savannah: French and American lines in the foreground. (Library of Congress)

RIGHT British camp in southern England. (The National Army Museum)

operation was successful, claiming the destruction and capture of more than 140 vessels and £2 million worth of goods and property, and the fleet returned triumphantly to New York on May 24.

Outside the Thirteen Colonies

The principal problem facing the British in 1779 was Spain's decision to enter the war. As described in the section on naval war (pp. 34–37), the naval balance shifted toward France and Spain as a result of this decision. Spain entered the war as an ally of the French, rather than of the Americans, on May 8; her main aim in doing so was to regain territory lost in the Seven Years' War. The British garrisons in western Florida were not aware of the Spanish entry, and so the British garrison at Baton Rouge was later seized in September 1779, an excellent

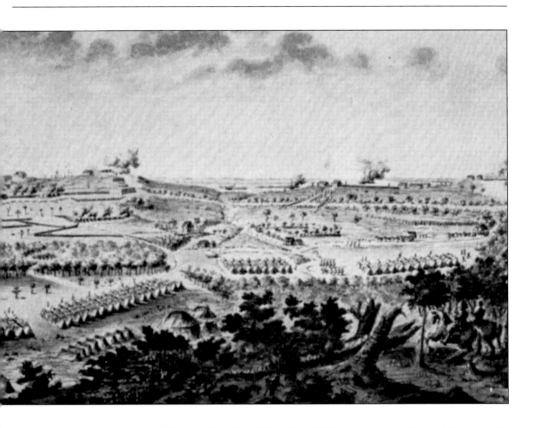

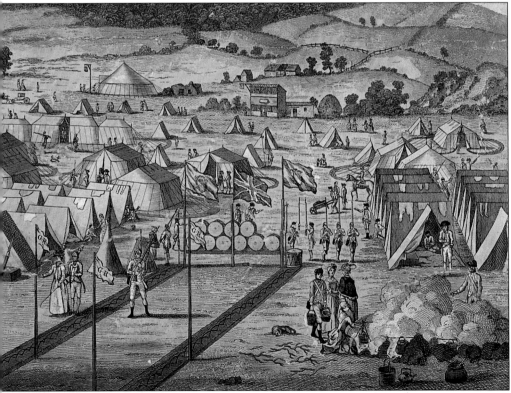

ABOVE Siege of Gibraltar. (Anne SK Brown Collection)

RIGHT The French capture of Grenada.
(The National Army Museum)

performance by the Spanish regulars and
Louisiana militia.

The combined forces of the Spanish and
French fleets gave the British Isles a fright
during the summer of 1779. A combined
force of 66 ships planned to assemble and
invade Great Britain. The Royal Navy was
aware of the potential threat, but had two
possible invasion sites to protect, southern
England and Ireland. On July 30, the
combined force, under the command of
Admiral d'Orvilliers, sailed from Brest,
picking up troops at Le Havre and St. Malo.
It appeared off Plymouth on August 16.
The British fleet, under the command of
Admiral Sir Charles Hardy, was out of
commission, stationed off Ireland. Local
militiamen were sent immediately to repel

any attempted landings by the estimated 30,000 enemy soldiers.

Despite its superiority in numbers, the Franco-Spanish fleet was apparently wary of attempting a landing, even before Hardy returned. A decisive British naval victory after the troops had been landed would potentially have left 30,000 troops stranded on the coast of England. The British fleet arrived with 39 ships in early September; Hardy refused to attack, preferring to await a move by the Franco-Spanish force. The invasion force decided to withdraw by mid-September; their ships were battered, the men growing tired and ill, and relations between the French and Spanish commanders had soured. Battle had been avoided, and the threat of invasion averted.

The first significant Spanish action upon entering the war was to lay siege to Gibraltar. Reinforcements were sent from Britain to support the British governor, George Augustus Elliott, although the first relief did not arrive until the beginning of 1780, under the command of Admiral Rodney. Gibraltar was under siege for the remainder of the war,

with relieving fleets entering to help the garrison stay alive.

The entry of Spain and France into the war threatened British interests in the West Indies and Central America. Before d'Estaing sailed for the ill-fated siege of Savannah, he had had several successes in the West Indies, capturing St. Vincent in mid-June and Grenada a month later. The British badly needed troops in the area, fearing an attack on Jamaica next. Luckily for them, nothing happened for the rest of the year, for they were unprepared to face it.

In India, the French post at Mahe fell in March 1779. Of more critical importance to the British, however, was the enmity that their actions provoked in Haidar Ali and his large army. His armies directly engaged the British, and continued to do so for the rest of the war.

By the end of 1779, the British military effort in North America had decidedly shifted toward the south. Prevost's defense of Savannah had sparked renewed interest in a southern campaign. General Clinton had been frustrated in his attempts to bring the Main Army to battle. The requirements of other theaters had made it clear that Clinton would not be able to rely on London for additional reinforcements. He therefore decided to abandon Newport, Rhode Island, and withdrew his force to New York. He assembled a large army in New York, and on December 26 embarked with more than 7,000 men for a campaign in South Carolina, with Charleston as his first objective. A large contingent of British troops remained in New York to protect the city, but the British post at Verplanck's Point was withdrawn. Washington had been having difficulty keeping his various armies together during the stalemate in the north. The campaign in the south over the course of 1780–81 would be decisive for the future of North America.

The land war: 1780–81

The land war in North America shifted to the southern colonies during the last phase of the war. The British generals, Clinton and Cornwallis, sought a decisive campaign in the south, believing that a large percentage of the population were loyalists. While maintaining a presence in New York, the British shifted their principal focus southward.

General Washington was having problems with his troops. The Main Army remained in the New York area to counteract British attempts to push into the Hudson River Valley or across New Jersey. The army's ability to wage war was limited by periodic mutinies, and the Southern Army bore the brunt of the fighting. The arrival of a large French contingent in 1780 enabled Washington to send the Main Army, bolstered by French reinforcements, south to Virginia. A classic siege at Yorktown followed, an incident that few foresaw might be the last major engagement of the war.

Southern campaign

In December 1779, General Henry Clinton left New York with more than 17,000 British troops, landing south of Charleston on February 11, 1780. The American commander, General Lincoln, received word that the British were accompanied by a large contingent of Carolina loyalist refugees. He thought that the British had another motive for their movements besides military conquest, "that of settling the country as they conquer" (Boston Public Library, G.380.38.207 b). The British, upon reaching Charleston, attempted to surround the town. Lincoln had 1,800 Continentals and about 2,000 militia to combat the British advance, and it was up to him to decide whether to engage in battle, withdraw, or hold out in the town. Ultimately, however, it was General Clinton who decided Charleston's fate.

By early April, British troops had crossed the northern routes of the town. A reinforcement of 700 Continentals arrived just after the town had been completely surrounded on April 14. The British began to dig siege lines and prepare artillery positions to bombard the defenders. Heavy fire was

Battle of Camden

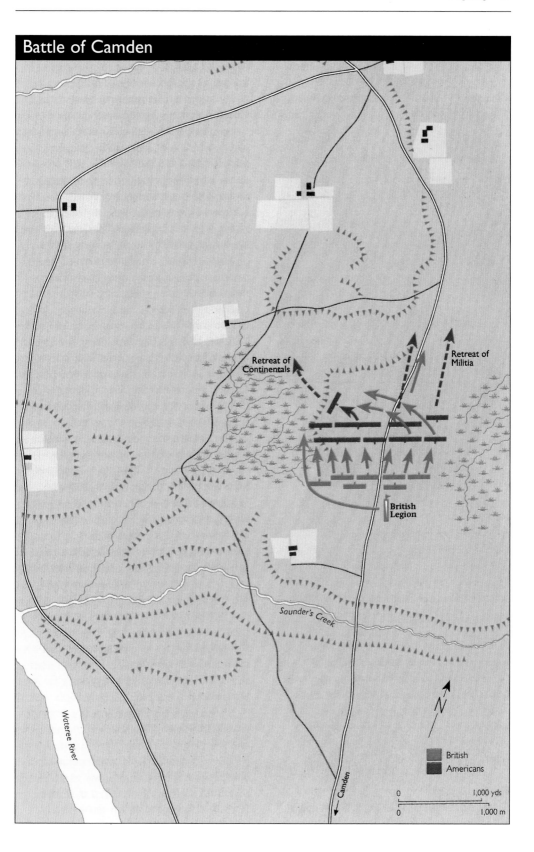

Retreat of
Continentals

Retreat of
Militia

British
Legion

Saunder's Creek

Wateree River

Camden

N

0   1,000 yds

0   1,000 m

British
Americans

Lieutenant General Earl Charles Cornwallis.
(Anne SK Brown Collection)

exchanged, but the British were able to dig a second line and position themselves within yards of the American lines. A Hessian officer, Captain Johaun Hinrichs reported that "the enemy stood our fire well and returned it till about noon ... but since our fire was so violent that we did not see them coming, they were compelled to withdraw. At two o'clock in the afternoon the enemy hoisted a large white flag" (*Siege of Charleston*, p. 289). An American observer recorded that, on May 12, "the Continental troops march out and pile their arms and the British take possession of the town" (G.380.20). This was the worst single defeat for the American forces during the war.

More than 2,000 Continental soldiers were captured, as well as 1,000 militia troops.

On May 29, the mixed loyalist force known as the British Legion and commanded by Lieutenant-Colonel Benastre Tarleton, having moved north from Charleston, destroyed a Virginia Continental force at Waxhaws. The American force was almost wiped out, and there is still debate about what happened when the Americans attempted to surrender, and whether Tarleton ordered the killing of prisoners. Either way, the Legion and Tarleton became synonymous with brutal fighting methods.

This incident, which occurred in the interior, sparked a command decision to move inland to suppress any subsequent civilian rebellion. On June 8, Clinton left Charleston with 4,000 troops to head to New York. He had received word that the French fleet and expeditionary force had arrived and feared that New York was a potential target. General Cornwallis took over command of the rest of the British forces in the south following his departure.

The British presence in South Carolina further inflamed the civil conflict already smoldering there. As the American General Moultrie noted, "Large armed parties of Whigs and Tories were continually moving about and frequently falling in with each other and fighting severe battles ... the animosities between the two parties were carried to great lengths ... to enumerate the cruelties which were exercised upon each other would fill a volume" (Moultrie, Vol. II, p. 219). Part of the reason for the increased hostility was a proclamation issued by Clinton before he left, demanding that all colonists must decide once and for all on whose side they were; no neutrality would be tolerated.

As the British marched into the interior, supply shortages created discipline problems, and the behavior of the British regulars won them few supporters. Cornwallis issued another proclamation, this one to the troops, regarding theft of cattle and provisions: "I do by this proclamation most strictly prohibit and forbid the same; and I do hereby give notice, that if any person offend herein ... [he] shall be further punished in a manner ... [that he] doth deserve" (Tarleton, pp. 121– 122).

General Lincoln was captured at Charleston and the hero of Saratoga, Major-General Horatio Gates, assumed command of the American forces in the south. He was able to rebuild the Southern Army with Continental soldiers from Maryland and Delaware and southern militiamen. His force consisted of only 1,500 Continentals and almost 1,000 militiamen. Gates arrived outside Camden, South Carolina, in early August. This was the main supply depot for the British forces in the interior, and Cornwallis, hearing of Gates' advance, had arrived with reinforcements from Charleston.

On the morning of August 16, the two armies clashed. The American left flank was composed of untrained militia units, with the Continentals on the right flank and in the rear of the first line. The British force moved forward and attacked the left flank first. Gates recorded that "at daylight the enemy attacked and drove in our light party in front, when I ordered the left to advance and attack the enemy; but to my astonishment, the left wing [Virginia militia] and North Carolina militia gave way" (Tarleton, p. 146). The Continentals fought hard. As Tarleton noted, "[Continental commander Baron de Kalbe] made a vigorous charge with a regiment of continental infantry through the left division of the British . . . after this last effort of the continentals, rout and slaughter ensued in every quarter" (Tarleton, p. 107). A second Southern Army had been badly defeated. Baron de Kalbe was killed and Gates fell from grace in the American command structure.

Following this victory, Cornwallis decided to push into North Carolina. He had failed to properly subdue South Carolina, however, and his communications and outposts were vulnerable to attack from militia forces as he advanced. Cornwallis marched into North

Carolina in early September, with a second column of provincial troops under the command of Major Patrick Ferguson on his left flank. Cornwallis and the main corps reached Charlotte, North Carolina, in late September. Ferguson moved further north with his corps but was unable to convince many loyalists in the area to join up; his destructive actions against rebels had aroused too much hatred.

On October 7, Ferguson's force of 800 men was surrounded at King's Mountain by a militia force of 2,000 expert forest-fighting men. Ferguson's force was 30 miles (48 km) from Cornwallis' column and could expect no support. A loyalist described how:

At about two o'clock in the afternoon, twenty five hundred rebels ... attacked us ... the action continued an hour and five minutes; but their numbers enabled them to surround us ... we had to surrender to save lives of the brave men who were left (Allaire, p. 31).

Baron de Kalbe. (New York Public Library)

A North American militiaman, James Collins, commented, "After the fight was over, the situation of the poor Tories appeared to be really pitiable; the dead lay in heaps on all sides, while the groans of the wounded were heard in every direction" (*Fire of Liberty*, p. 200). The British force was completely destroyed, forcing Cornwallis to withdraw to South Carolina for winter quarters and lowering the morale of southern loyalists.

The American Southern Army was re-formed while Cornwallis spent the winter south of Camden, South Carolina. He was to be reinforced by a contingent under Major-General Alexander Leslie, who had been undertaking raids in Virginia. Command of the American Southern Army was given to Major-General Nathaniel Greene on December 2, 1780. He had another force of 1,000 Continental troops and various militia forces at his disposal. The fighting in the backcountry between rebels and loyalists continued unabated throughout the winter months.

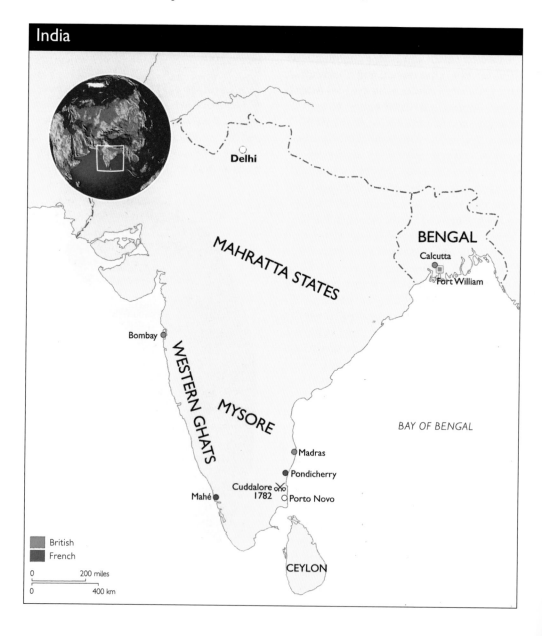

India

Delhi

BENGAL

Calcutta

Fort William

MAHRATTA STATES

Bombay

WESTERN GHATS

MYSORE

BAY OF BENGAL

Madras

Pondicherry

Cuddalore
1782

Mahé

Porto Novo

■ British
■ French

0   200 miles
0   400 km

CEYLON

In January 1781, Cornwallis decided to march back into North Carolina. General Green dispatched Brigadier Daniel Morgan and a small Continental corps to disrupt the British lines of communication and fight in the backcountry. Cornwallis dispatched a force of the British Legion and other troops, under the command of Lieutenant-Colonel Tarleton, in a mobile force to protect the left flank of the British forces and counteract Morgan's corps.

Morgan's and Tarleton's forces clashed north of Cowpens, on the border between North and South Carolina, on January 17. Morgan deployed his riflemen at the front of his force, with the militia and Continentals forming the second and third lines. The riflemen were to shoot once, then withdraw through the ranks of the other lines. The battle began at daylight, with Tarleton sending his tired troops immediately into battle. The American riflemen created holes in the British line as it advanced. The British pushed forward and the Americans, militia, and riflemen began to pull back. The British surged forward and the Americans turned and delivered a heavy volley. The British attack fell apart as the Continental troops moved forward. Tarleton and a few hundred men were able to escape, but the force had lost more than 700 men killed and captured.

The reasons for Tarleton's defeat were twofold. First, Morgan had deployed well and was able to shift his forces without much disruption. Second, as loyalist officer Alescambe Chesney noted: "We suffered a dreadful defeat by some dreadful bad management ... the rout was almost total" (Add. Mss. 32627). The Legion was an important asset for the British forces and, in one battle, Cornwallis had lost nearly all of it.

Cornwallis continued his advance into North Carolina after reinforcements arrived from General Leslie, and the American and British forces met again on March 15 at Guildford Court House in North Carolina. Cornwallis had only 2,000 troops; the Southern Army outnumbered him two to one. General Greene, however, elected to

Brigadier Nathaniel Greene. (Anne SK Brown Collection)

take the defensive. The Americans were drawn up as "three lines: the front line was composed of North Carolina militia ... second line of the Virginia militia ... third line, consisting of two brigades, one of Virginia, and one of Maryland continentals troops" (Tarleton, p. 314).

The battle lasted for three hours. The first line of North Carolina militia fired once before breaking. The Virginia militia stood longer, delivering strong volleys. The British dealt with the first two lines of militia and turned toward the Continental troops. The British continued to press and, though suffering heavily, began to break the Maryland Continentals, causing the American right flank to falter, after British artillery fired into the confusing mass. As Greene reported: "The engagement was long and severe, and the enemy only gained their point by superior discipline" (Tarleton, p. 316).

The British lost some 100 men killed and more than 400 wounded. The American forces lost only 78 killed and nearly 200 wounded. It was a Pyrrhic victory for

Cornwallis, and afterward he headed south to Wilmington to rendezvous with the Royal Navy and receive much-needed supplies and reinforcements. Greene turned toward South Carolina.

While in Wilmington, Cornwallis had to decide whether to move into Virginia or to return by sea to Charleston. Brigadier Greene had moved into South Carolina, while General Lord Rawdon and his troops attempted to hold parts of the interior centered around Camden and Fort Ninety-Six. Greene attacked Lord Rawdon outside Camden, at Hobkirk's Hill, on April 25; the British were able to defeat the American force. On the same day, Cornwallis and his force marched toward Virginia.

The remainder of the campaign in the Carolinas was one of gradual withdrawal for the British forces. On May 10, the British pulled out of Camden, and by June, the only post in the interior still in British hands was Fort Ninety-Six. Greene laid siege to it, but was forced by a British relief column to lift the siege. The British, however, recognizing the distance from Charleston to Fort Ninety-Six, subsequently withdrew from the area, and by mid-summer they controlled only the coastal strip from Savannah to Charleston. Greene had lost many of the battles, but in the end he won the campaign in the Carolinas.

Virginia and Yorktown

Cornwallis countermanded orders from London that his troops were to remain in the Carolinas. British troops had already been stationed in Virginia to stage raids in the area and relieve pressure on the British forces in the Carolinas. Virginia was intended to be a secondary campaign, but Cornwallis turned it into a primary operation without receiving approval from London or Clinton in New York. Cornwallis' actions clearly demonstrate the friction that had arisen among senior generals in North America. As a result of his decision, the operation in Virginia became the decisive campaign.

In January 1781, a British force of 1,500 troops was dispatched by Clinton to

Virginia, commanded by Benedict Arnold, the former American general. Arnold had switched sides in 1780 because he felt that he was being sidelined by Congress and the Continental Army. He had been commander of an important American post, West Point, on the Hudson River. General Clinton had negotiated with him to turn over plans of the strategic fort to the British, but the plot was uncovered before it could be implemented. Arnold escaped to New York and was given command of a British force in the rank of major-general.

In March 1781, a second British force of 2,000 men, under the command of Major-General William Phillips, arrived in

Major-General Benedict Arnold. (Anne SK Brown Collection)

Virginia. General Phillips assumed command of all British troops in Virginia upon his arrival, and continued the raids in Virginia. Cornwallis arrived in mid-May and met with Phillips at Petersburg, Virginia. The combined British force now totaled more than 7,000 men and was under the overall command of Cornwallis, who took over after Philips died of typhoid fever. The American commanders in the region, Major-Generals de Lafayette and von Steuben, had been focusing on trying to increase the numbers of Continental troops while contending with two earlier campaigns staged by Arnold and Phillips.

As Cornwallis arrived, the American forces withdrew from the southern areas of Virginia. The two armies met and skirmished. The mixed-force British irregular units, the British Legion and Queen's Rangers, ranged far and wide, carrying out raids throughout the southern area of the colony. Cornwallis set out to trap and destroy the American forces through a series of maneuvers, but was unsuccessful, and the British withdrew toward Williamsburg in late June. Cornwallis received orders to embark 3,000 troops for New York. He withdrew toward the James River at Greenspring Farm. Lafayette followed up his withdrawal, and Cornwallis defeated a small American corps that reached Greenspring Farm on July 6. Cornwallis then withdrew toward Portsmouth, where he received word that his troops were to remain in Virginia.

By early July, Cornwallis had received orders to establish a fortified winter base for the Royal Navy. Yorktown was chosen as a suitable site, and by the beginning of August, the British had begun the work of fortifying the area and the adjoining Gloucester Point. In doing so, the British had committed themselves to a defensive position, and the American forces stationed in Virginia began to close in on Yorktown.

The year 1780 and winter of 1781 was a difficult time for General Washington and the Main Army. In the spring of 1780, the Main Army stood at 4,000 men and was suffering from lack of supplies. Discipline was an increasing problem as the war in the north became ever more hopelessly stalemated. In May, troops from the Connecticut regiments threatened to march into New Jersey and seize stores. They were restrained from doing so by other troops, principally the Pennsylvania regiments. Ironically, in January 1781, elements of the Pennsylvania regiments themselves mutinied, this time over supplies and timely pay. The issue of delayed pay was exacerbated by the fact that the money issued by the Continental Congress was rapidly being devalued. At the end of January, elements of the New Jersey regiments also mutinied. All three revolts collapsed, and the ringleaders were found and punished, but it was clear that the Main Army was in need of a campaign.

Washington benefited at this stage from the arrival of a French expeditionary force of 5,000 troops that landed in Newport in 1780, under the command of Lieutenant-General Rochambeau. They were subsequently reinforced in Virginia with an additional 3,000 men. With Cornwallis heading toward Yorktown, the Main Army and the French expeditionary force on August 14 decided to wage a campaign against Cornwallis. Proposed attacks against New York had to be rejected due to the lack of French naval support so far north, as the French Admiral de Grasse had agreed to go only as far north as the Chesapeake River.

The joint American and French force, numbering more than 8,000 French and 2,000 Continentals in the summer, marched south, but in a deceptive manner. More than 4,000 Continentals and 2,000 militia remained in New York, intending to keep the pressure on Clinton while concealing from Cornwallis that Yorktown was their eventual destination. The French troops provided an important dimension to the American contingent; they were regular troops, trained and disciplined to deal with the likes of the British Redcoats. With the addition of more than 5,000 Continental troops and a large artillery train, the British forces faced a solid opponent. The naval engagement at the Capes, an entrance to Chesapeake Bay, in early September, although not significant in terms

French troops landing at Newport. (New York Public Library)

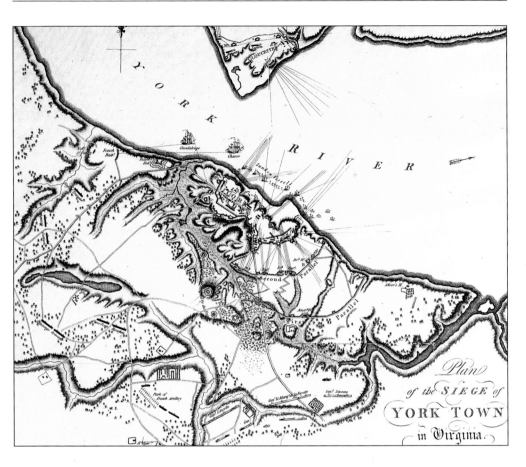

ABOVE Siege of Yorktown: the American and French positions are to the south and west of Yorktown. Redoubts 9 and 10 are listed as A and B to the southeast of Yorktown. (Bodleian Library)

BELOW Surrender of Yorktown. (Anne SK Brown Collection)

of ships damaged, became decisive when the British Admiral Thomas Graves withdrew to New York, isolating Cornwallis.

The main American and French forces gathered in Williamsburg on September 26. The American forces numbered over 8,000 men, while the French numbered over 8,000 men. The Continental Army marched toward Yorktown in three columns of troops, two French and one American. As a French officer noted, "We arrived about six o'clock that evening [September 28] before the town of Yorktown and immediately began to invest it" (Rice and Brown, p. 57). The siege of Yorktown followed the practices of any European-style siege: both sides embarked on raids and fired artillery at redoubts and trenches. A French officer commented that "the day was spent in cannonading and firing bombs at each other in such profusion that we did one another much damage" (Rice and Brown, p. 59).

The French and American engineers dug their trenches, progressing closer to the British positions, and the siege increasingly centered on the taking of two British redoubts, nos. 9 and 10. On the evening of October 14, the French and American troops launched an attack on the redoubts. The French commander, William Count de Deux-Ponts, detailed the attack and, although uncommunicative to a degree, noted that firing took place during the French attack. He stated:

The first fifty les chausseurs [light infantry] carried fascines, of the other fifty there were only eight who carried ladders, after them came the grenadiers ... [They] advanced with the greatest silence .... [and] opened fire ... we lost not a moment in reaching the abbatis ... [It] was cleared away with brave determination ... I gave the order to fire ... the enemy kept up a sharp fire ... our fire increasing and making terrible havoc among the enemy (Deux-Ponts, pp. 145–146).

On October 16 a sortie of 300 men was launched from the British lines to destroy and spike the guns in two allied artillery batteries. The undertaking was considered a success, yet the guns were firing again within six hours of the attack. As Cornwallis noted, "the action, though extremely honorable to the officers and soldiers who executed it, proved of little public advantage" (Tarleton, p. 429).

On October 19, Cornwallis surrendered the garrison at Yorktown. The British garrison troops marched out and laid down their arms, flanked by the American army on one side and the French army on the other. Clinton had intended to send a relieving force of 7,000 men, but news arrived that Cornwallis had already surrendered before he could do so.

The battle for Yorktown was the last major engagement of the land war in North America, but the war was not yet over. The British were still fighting a war outside the North American theater, and had not intended Yorktown to be the last major engagement on American soil. The Americans, for their part, had plans to drive the British garrisons out of both Charleston and New York. Other considerations for the French prevented the launch of attacks on British forces stationed on the coast of the Carolinas, or Georgia, or in New York. After Yorktown, the war shifted almost completely to the West Indies, India, Florida, and Europe.

Massachusetts professional

The soldier discussed in this section was called Benjamin Gould. There are no dates for his age or for the year that he died. His story originates from a manuscript written in his own hand at the end of the war. It provides an interesting account of an American soldier of the period who served during the siege of Boston, as well as in operations in New York City and near Saratoga.

Gould begins his story with his enlistment in Captain John Beecher's company, which was part of Colonel Moses Little's regiment. Little's regiment is listed as a Continental infantry regiment. No date is provided, but Gould's regiment was part of the army that occupied Boston following the British withdrawal on March 17, 1776. Gould claims that he joined the army as a sergeant. If this is true, then he must have had previous military experience as a private soldier, although he does not provide any background information.

Gould's regiment was ordered to New York City as the threat to that area increased. He describes how his regiment arrived in the New York area just as battle began on Long Island: "In the morning we heard a heavy cannonading … it was the enemy, taking Long Island and New York and our army retreating from it." Following the defeat on Long Island, his regiment was ordered to proceed to Fort Washington, on Manhattan Island. His regiment was ordered to make carriages and to supply the fort with additional material in preparation for a possible siege. The regiment arrived as the artillery began preparations for the British arrival.

Gould comments that supplies ran low during the regiment's tenure at Fort Washington. He reports when Royal Navy ships appeared off the west side of the fort on the Hudson and records that a detachment of British troops was reported

to be only 3 miles (5 km) from the fort. He states that "[we] could not spare a man to draw provisions and [were] obliged to live upon potatoes and cloves for several days." Instead of attacking right away, however, the main British force headed north to White Plains in an attempt to catch the Main Continental Army.

It is at this point that the manuscript becomes somewhat confusing. Up to now, Gould described his regiment as if it were an infantry unit. His parent regiment, Little's, Massachusetts Battalion, is listed as an infantry formation in 1775 under the command of Brigadier Nathaniel Greene's brigade. The manuscript, however, raises the possibility that Gould had been transferred to an artillery unit. He describes orders "to make the best grape [shot] I could." Also, his regiment was ordered to proceed to White Plains to support the Main Army. His subsequent description of the battle of White Plains supports the theory that he fought with an artillery unit, especially when he describes how "when our army retreated I struck the left tent and took the last cannon from our lines."

This description ends the narrative of the 1776 campaign. Gould mentions the ongoing problem of keeping the numbers of men in the Continental service constant for a long period of time. At the end of 1776, his own Continental service comes to an end, and he is offered service with the Massachusetts militia, with the proviso that he could "leave at anytime for service with the Continentals if he wished." He notes, "taken from the Continental Service and placed in the militia in the summer of 1777." His new militia unit was sent to fight against the British advance down Lake Champlain and along the Hudson, but he does not make it clear in which of the

British caricature of American soldiers at Boston—not an accurate depiction. (The British Museum)

several Massachusetts militia regiments involved in this campaign he served.

Gould's unit most likely arrived during the month of September when, as described earlier, American units were operating behind Burgoyne's line of advance to disrupt his supply networks. His unit was given four days' supplies and ordered to operate on Lake George. American forces had seized Fort George on September 18, and from there they had pushed north to Fort Ticonderoga. Gould's unit operated in the area around Lake George "for 17 days." His narrative is unclear, but it appears that his unit marched south toward Bemis Heights, since he next describes a major action on the 7th (presumably of October, when an engagement took place at that location). Although he was with a unit of Massachusetts militia, they are not specifically mentioned in accounts of the battle. Massachusetts Continental regiments and various New England militia units were present, however, and his unit may have been attached to one of these groups for the battle.

Gould describes how, on "the seventh [of October], at about one o'clock, we were laid by

the cannon of the enemy who were marching to attack us." He appears to be describing the last British attack against Bemis Heights on October 7. He goes on to record that:

We returned to our places and was immediately ordered to march … it was but a few minutes before the enemy fired upon us … a second shot; our men seemed terrified at this but soon received and stood their ground nobley [sic] … the enemy made no refrain but retreated precipitately.

He also describes coming across an abandoned British camp and his actions:

"I took nothing out of it but a bottle of beer which was very exceptible [sic] as we were very dry."

Gould's unit was given its discharge on November 1, 1777, but he stayed in the area to settle accounts. He next refers to 1780, when he notes receiving command of a militia company. This implies that he received a commission, either after the Battle of Bemis Heights or when he was called up for the militia in 1780. Gould and his company were ordered to West Point; they arrived there on June 20, 1780, and he spent the remainder of his service on garrison duty at West Point. He was discharged at the end of the conflict.

War on the homefront

Impact on local populations

Although the war was economically costly for all sides, it differed significantly from the Seven Years' War in that the impact on the local populations was relatively minimal. The home populations of France, Great Britain, and Spain did not suffer under foreign occupation. Large numbers of troops were raised in each country and inevitably created tension and damage by the fact of their presence, but they were not occupying forces. The large number of troops even proved an unintended boon to the British government when the Gordon Riots of 1780 broke out, and the armed forces were used to restore law and order.

The fighting in the West Indies and India undoubtedly created problems between the local populations and the various armies. The numerous and powerful cavalry of Haidar Ali set out to destroy the communications and supplies of the East India Company armies, which left civilians caught between two armies. As with all campaigns in the region, soldiers deserted from one side to the other as economic conditions dictated.

The Thirteen American colonies suffered the most when measuring impact on the civilian populations. Both sides, including the French Army, were guilty of abuses and maltreatment of the civilian population. The behavior of the French Army in 1780–81 was exemplary in its restraint from plundering and looting, but the French force that invested Savannah in 1779 was not so commendable. The Americans and French eventually formed a special mixed unit of French and American dragoons to police both armies (see Boston Public Library, G.380.38.1.60b, 30/9/1779).

The British and their German auxiliaries were consistently accused of pillaging, raping, and general disorder by the colonists. The British advance across New Jersey in 1776 was considered a particularly brutal episode. An American observer described how:

familys ... escape[d] from the Regular Army and left a Great Part of their goods behind them in their Houses for want of carriages to take them away, Great part of which fell into the Regular hands, and they not only burnt up all the fire wood ... [but] stript shops, out houses, and some dwelling houses (Collins, p. 4).

Many British regulars considered the conflict as a rebellion, and consequently had minimal sympathy for the civilians.

The German auxiliaries' attitude was similarly contemptuous. Lieutenant-Colonel Kemble of the 60th Foot noted on October 3, 1776, that "ravages committed by the Hessians, and all the Ranks of the Army, on the poor inhabitants of the country make their case deplorable" (Kemble, p. 91). Kemble also succinctly described the effects of these actions: "The country all this time unmercifully Pillaged by our troops, Hessians in particular, no wonder if the Country people refuse to join us" (Kemble, p. 96).

Senior British commanders attempted to confront this issue, but it was never conclusively resolved. As previously described, a series of proclamations was written and distributed amongst the troops at the onset of the 1780–81 southern campaign, in an attempt to forestall some of the problems. The British Army's supply problems complicated the situation and more or less condoned this sort of behavior; units were sent out on foraging parties to round up cattle and other supplies. They were supposed to pay for the items, but of course abuse was common. Naval landings were carried out specifically to steal and

The burning of New York. British soldiers apprehend and deal roughly with suspected rebels who were blamed for starting the fires. (The British Museum)

destroy stores that could be destined for the Continental Army, with inevitable repercussions for civilians. The civilian populations of New Jersey and southern New York and New England were at the mercy of the British raiding parties.

The regions around New York and southern New England also suffered from their proximity to encampments of the Continental Army. There were cases of outright robbery and abuse by troops on the civilian population. As the various armies marched across New Jersey in 1776 and 1777, the countryside was stripped bare of food and supplies. The Continental Army and militia also carried out attacks on suspected loyalist families in the area. Their properties were looted and, depending upon the local commander, certain members of the family were killed. An American private soldier commented that in 1780 "there was a large number [of loyalists] in this place and its vicinity by the name of Hetfield who were notorious rascals," and who escaped. The soldier went on, "thus these murderous

villains escaped the punishment due to their infernal deeds" (Martin, pp. 180–181). There were critics of this policy within the American high command. Major-General Israel Putnam commented in August 1777, in response to a local assembly motion from Salem, Massachusetts, to confiscate lands of suspected loyalists: "I think such things are counter to the spirit of your resolves" (Boston Public Library, Ch.F.7.85).

The southern campaign raised the level of violence within the civilian population to outright civil war. The fighting in the backcountry lasted from the official outbreak of war until well after the siege of Yorktown. The British Army's practices and fighting tactics, as with the war in the north, turned neutrals into rebels. The American Brigadier-General William Moultrie described the march of the British regulars and "their severities against the unhappy citizens, many of whom they hung up or otherwise cruelly treated ... the war was carried with great barbarity" (Moultrie, Vol. II, p. 219). Lieutenant-Colonel Tarleton's view of the civilian population counters this: "The foraging parties were every day harassed by the inhabitants ... [They] generally fired from covert places, to annoy the British detachments" (Tarleton, p. 160). The conflict turned into an irregular war in the south, and abuses were perpetrated by both sides. A loyalist reported how "a Henry Meholm, an old man of 81 years of age, this day met us ... [He] had walked upwards of an hundred miles [160 km] ... his errand was to get some kind of assistance. He had been plundered by the Rebels, and stripped of everything" (Allaire, p. 19).

Trade and economy

The economic costs of the war were heavy for Great Britain. The average yearly cost of the war was £12 million. The Royal Navy was not able to control the seas as she had done in the Seven Years' War. Taxes on the general population increased as the war dragged on, and duties on items not already being taxed were imposed to increase revenue further. The average land tax during the war was established at four shillings for every pound (Conway, p. 189), and the government borrowed heavily to make up for the shortfalls. This load of debt was added to the outstanding debts amassed during the Seven Years' War.

Trade also suffered as a result of the war. The revenue raised from trade with the Thirteen Colonies was wiped away. The merchants who traded with the American colonies felt the pinch, especially those in the tobacco trade. The export market was also hit hard. The revenue raised from the selling of woolen and metal goods dropped sharply as the markets dried up. The incursion of France and Spain into the war increased the pressure on Britain's import and export trade as more markets dried up due to naval pressure and privateering.

The need to increase shipping to get provisions and troops to North America prompted the Admiralty to lease a significant number of merchant ships. This provided additional opportunities for American privateers and Spanish and French fleet seizures, causing further disruption. It is estimated that 3,386 British merchant ships were seized during the war (Conway, p. 191). The British were able to recoup some of these losses with their own privateering efforts on Spanish and French shipping.

The war did provide some benefit for a number of industries in Great Britain. The expansion of the navy and army meant an increased demand for the supplies needed to build ships, outfit troops, and supply forces in North America. Overall, however, the import and export trade fell drastically, creating significant revenue problems for the British government.

The American colonies also suffered economically as a result of the war. At first, the war increased prosperity; the trade of the Thirteen Colonies was no longer restricted to Great Britain, and merchants could trade throughout Europe and the West Indies without the interference of Royal Customs officials. American privateering activities infused additional wealth into the cause. As the fighting dragged on, however, American resources became strained as shipping was destroyed or seized by Royal Navy raids.

Ironically, the Americans' biggest financial problems concerned the imposition of taxes to raise currency. Individual colonies fought to keep the right to vote on tax issues, and the Continental Congress was forced to accept that they would not be given the power to raise taxes. Coin circulation had proved insufficient to keep the war going as early as 1775. The Congress turned to the establishment of paper money or bills of credit to raise funds. The expansion of the economy during the first two years of the war allowed for paper money to be infused into the economy without any problems. As the war continued and the costs rose, however, both the Congress and the colonies continued to print money, creating enormous inflation problems.

By 1780, the Congress and colonies combined had issued over $400 million in paper money, and inflation had skyrocketed. In an attempt to stop the inflation, the Congress tried to impose reforms, but these succeeded only in devaluing the Congress' dollars. The Congress also asked the colonies to fund, equip, and outfit their own troops in the Continental Army. The European allies also gave the Americans nearly $10 million in loans to keep the war effort afloat, but by 1780 there was widespread disaffection within the army over issues of pay and supplies. As Colonel Tallmadge noted: "The pay to the army being entirely in continental paper, we were greatly embarrassed to procure even the necessary supplies of food and clothing" (Tallmadge, p. 33). The inflation and debts produced by the war were to plague the newly formed United States for a number of years.

France, like Great Britain, piled debts from this war on those still outstanding from the Seven Years' War. French debt at the end of the war stood at 3,315.1 million *livres* (Conway, p. 242), spent in developing a sizeable army and navy, and providing material support to the American cause. This debt created significant economic problems after the war. In fact, many historians contend that the debt incurred during both the Seven Years' War and the American Revolution, compounded by the financial crisis of 1786, were among the principal causes of the French Revolution.

Spain also suffered, but not as greatly as France. Spain nearly doubled her spending from 454 million *reales* in 1778 to over 700 million *reales* in 1779 (Lynch, p. 326). Then the conflict disrupted the revenue stream from South and Central America. Spain at first sought more taxes, but when this did not solve the issue, royal bonds were issued to make up the shortfall. This did not work either, and finally, in 1782, the first national Bank of Spain—the Banco San Carlos—was created to centralize financial efforts. When the war finally ended, the revenue from the colonies came into the bank to help pay off the loans and bonds during the war years, enabling Spain to pay off most of her debts relatively quickly.

Boston loyalist

A series of letters written from 1768 to 1776 by a female loyalist in Boston provide insight into the political agitation of the time in general, and the state of affairs in Boston in particular. Most of the letters were written to friends in Great Britain, and provide a different perspective on the "patriots" or "rebels" than the images commonly portrayed. Her brother, Henry Hulton, was the Commissioner of Customs for His Majesty's Government in Boston. In late 1775, Mrs. Hulton left for Britain as a loyalist refugee. Her letters are then written to a friend, but they incorporate information conveyed to her by her brother regarding the siege of Boston. There is no information regarding her age, but she was most likely of middle age during the 1770s. She died in Britain in 1790.

In a letter dated January 31, 1774, Mrs. Hulton describes the brutal practice of "tarring and feathering." Many people who were loyalists or government officials were subjected to this treatment by radical elements of the rebel cause. This letter was written before General Gage arrived with a large contingent of troops and describes how:

The most shocking cruelty was exercised a few nights ago, upon a poor old man and tidesman one Malcolm ... [A] quarrell was picked with him, he was afterward taken and tarred and feathered ... they gave him several severe whippings at different parts of town (January 1774).

She also notes the aftermath of the attack: "The doctors say that it is impossible this poor creature can live, they say his flesh comes off his back in stakes" (January 1774).

A letter from March 1774 vividly portrays the mindset within Boston, even as the

British troops arrive. It is clear that the loyalists felt besieged and were awaiting the British troops to impose law and order. Mrs. Hulton describes the city:

[Boston] is a very gloomy place, the streets almost empty, many families have removed from it, and the inhabitants are divided into several parties at variance and quarrelling with each other. Some appear disponding, others full of rage ... those who are well disposed toward government are termed tories, they daily increase and have made some effects to take power out of the hands of the patriots, but they are intimidated and overpowered by [their] numbers. (March 1774)

She also states: "I don't despair of seeing peace and tranquillity in America tho they [patriots] talk very high and furious at present. They [patriots] are preparing their arms and ammunition and say if any of the leaders are seized and they will make reprisals on the friends of the government" (March 1774).

The next letter is dated a year later, after the British advance and battles at Lexington and Concord. Mrs. Hulton attempts to describe the fighting on April 19, including one particular incident that clearly demonstrates how misinformation occurs and subsequently provokes retaliation. Near the bridge at Concord, a young American boy hacked a wounded British soldier with an axe. It appears that the young boy overreacted with fear when the British soldier stirred. British troops, returning, saw a soldier with an axe wound to the head, and the rumor quickly circulated that the soldier had been scalped, an Indian custom considered brutal and barbaric. Hearing and believing this false information, many British soldiers retreating to Boston took vengeance on captured "patriots." Mrs. Hulton told an even worse tale: "Two or three of their people [British Redcoats] lying with agonies of death scalped and their noses cut off and eyes bored out ... which exasperated the soldiers exceedingly" (April 1775).

Writing from Great Britain in January 1776, Mrs. Hulton described the state of Boston, passing along information from her brother, who had remained with his family. He told of how "provisions and fuel were scarce and very dear, supplies once certain, temperatures weather and the winter get very severe ... amidst all this alarms dangers and distresses the small pox spread universally" (January 1776).

Mrs. Hulton's last letter, dated February 1776, documents the condition of Boston on the eve of the evacuation, as well as two instances of attacks on suspected loyalists. Accounts of the attacks may be slightly exaggerated, but they are not dissimilar to stories told by "patriot" forces describing the behavior of loyalists or British/German troops in North America. In Boston, "the poor soldiers endured great hardships and fatigues, deluged with rain, then chilled with frost, whilest they are in their tents without straw."

She related one action by "patriots": "The cruelties which are exercised on all those who are in their [patriots'] power is shocking, by advice from Kennebec, the committee there sentenced a man to be buried alive for wishing success to the King's troops, and that action had been executed upon him." Even more disturbing was a story originating in Roxbury [outside Boston]: Mr. Ed Brindley's wife, whilst laying in, had a squad of rebels always in her room who treated her with great rudeness and indecency, exposing her to view their banditti as a sight "see a Tory woman" and stripped her and her children of their linen and clothes (February 1776).

Mrs. Hulton's brother was evacuated with the British contingent from Boston to Halifax. He wrote to his sister from there in June 1776. His letter sums up the fate of many of those who had sided with the British government or were suspected of loyalist sympathies: "We suffer a loss of property with many worthy persons, here [in Halifax] alas are many families who lived in ease and plenty in Boston that now have scarce a shelter or any means of substance" (June 1776).

Stalemate

As noted previously, the British Army presence in North America was drastically reduced after 1778 and received reinforcements on only a few subsequent occasions. The vast majority of the army was deployed to contend with threats elsewhere in the world. France was able to deliver a large expeditionary force to North America in 1780 that performed successfully in Virginia, but the remainder of the French forces posed an effective threat to British interests elsewhere. Most French troops earmarked for overseas duty were sent to the West Indies, but a sizeable force was also sent to aid the Spanish in the Minorca and Gibraltar campaigns. Another five regiments were sent to fight in India, and the remainder of the army stayed in France, posing a continuing threat to the British Isles. The Spanish land forces, although not as well equipped or trained as their French or British counterparts, provided an additional headache for the British outposts in the Floridas and Caribbean.

The West Indies and the Caribbean

The first major land engagements in the West Indies occurred in 1781, after a series of indecisive naval engagements during 1780. Following a declaration of war on the Dutch Republic in late December 1780, the British moved against the Dutch colony of St. Eustatius and seized it on February 3, 1781. Tensions between neutral states and the British had been exacerbated by Royal Navy seizures of neutral shipping. The Dutch had carried on trade with the Thirteen Colonies throughout the war, and Russia and the Scandinavian states had begun to form a "League of Armed Neutrality" to protect

their shipping from the various belligerents. Britain feared that the powerful Dutch naval and merchant fleet would also join, and decided to attack them before they could do so. British aggression put Dutch colonies throughout the world at risk.

The defeat of Cornwallis at Yorktown freed the French Admiral de Grasse to return to the West Indies in December 1781. The French land forces were led by Marquis de Bouille, governor of Martinigue. The French moved against the British-occupied island of St. Lucia. On May 10, the French landed on the island, but upon deciding that the British defensive works were too strong, they re-embarked. The British force holding St. Eustatius was defeated by a French force on November 26, and St. Martin and St. Bartholomew fell in quick succession. The British island of St. Kitts became the next target, and on January 11, 1782, 6,000 men landed on the island and launched a siege. On February 13, the British surrendered the island. The French also seized Monserat and Nevis in February 1782.

This success encouraged the French and Spanish to attempt an assault on Jamaica. However, their incursion was so vigorously rebuffed by the British Admiral Rodney, at the battle of the Saintes, that they decided to call off the invasion. Instead, the Spanish turned their efforts to the British islands in the Bahamas, whose small British garrisons were easily overwhelmed by 5,000 Spanish troops. Rochambeau's expeditionary force was ordered to the Caribbean in the winter of 1782–83 in preparation for another attempt on Jamaica, but the fighting in the Caribbean slowed down during 1783, when news arrived that peace negotiations had begun. The last operation was conducted by British provincial units from Florida, who seized parts of the Bahama Islands in April 1783.

Of secondary importance to the fighting in the West Indies were the campaigns in Honduras, Nicaragua, and the Floridas between British and Spanish forces. A small force of regulars, provincial troops from Jamaica, and sailors seized the Spanish base at Bacalar, on the Honduran coast, on October 20, 1779. Sickness followed, soon driving the British out of the area and back to Jamaica. In 1780, the British decided to move against the Spanish establishment in Nicaragua, and a force was sent against the San Juan river area and Lake Nicaragua. The expedition, successful at first, was soon bogged down by disease and lack of supplies. As the British commander, Lieutenant-Colonel Stephen Kemble, noted: "Should the sickness continue, [it would] absolutely put an end to our pushing forward" (8010-32-1). An officer in the Jamaica corps also noted: "Sickness is rampant" (8010-32-3). Sickness also occured in the Spanish forces, but not to provoke a surrender sufficiently. The British were forced to withdraw most of the troops, and the remaining small British force was easily overwhelmed before the end of the year.

The Spanish, led by Bernardo de Galvez, had great success against the British garrisons in the Floridas. They set out to take the British garrisons at Mobile and Pensacola, and took Mobile on March 14. After a year's activity, the Spanish moved toward Pensacola in early 1781. The siege of Pensacola was a joint Franco-Spanish effort of some 7,000 men, against a British garrison of only two regular regiments plus assorted provincial corps units. The Franco-Spanish force began to envelop the town in March 1781, commencing a siege that would last for close to two months. A Spanish observer, noting the supply problems, commented: "That afternoon [May 6] the general told me of the great difficulty in which he found himself ... not enough [cannonballs] to supply the batteries ... almost all the cannonballs fired by the enemy were gathered up" (Saavedra, p. 168). Nevertheless, the British surrendered on May 9. The reason given for the surrender was that "a shell from one of our howitzers

Battle of Pensacola. (Anne SK Brown Collection)

Frederik William Augustus, Baron von Steuben.
(Anne SK Brown Collection)

fell into the powder magazine ... the
majority of the soldiers had perished in the
explosion" (Saavedra, p. 171).

Europe

The initial threat to Britain of invasion from
France had receded somewhat after the joint
Franco-Spanish fleet had returned to port
in France and Spain at the end of 1779, but
it was still not possible for the British to
release ships or soldiers for duty in other
areas. The attentions of France and Spain
were principally focused on Minorca and
Gibraltar, but the Channel Islands were still
in danger. A second French attempt to
invade the islands took place in January
1781, and St. Helier was seized. The British
retaliated and recaptured the island.

The fight for Gibraltar centered on the
ability of the British to reinforce and
resupply the garrison. The Spanish and
French were able to lay siege effectively, but

were unable to completely seal off the port
or destroy all the relief fleets coming out
from Britain. The British garrison was having
a difficult time though. A Spanish officer
commented, regarding a Hanoverian
deserter, "Scurvy makes great ravages
among the men ... [They] are extremely
fatigued" (5701-9). The siege continued
throughout the course of the war, but the
British never gave in.

During the summer of 1781, a
Franco-Spanish fleet attempted to seize the
British island of Minorca. On August 19,
1781, 8,000 troops landed and laid siege to
the British Fort St. Philip. The siege dragged
on until February 1782, when the British
surrendered the island and the garrison.

India

As noted previously, the British dispatched
the French forces quickly in 1778, but then
had to deal with the large armies of Haidar
Ali. The British fought a series of four wars,
called the Mysore Wars, with Haidar Ali and
his son, Tipu Sultan. Haidar Ali and his army
attacked the Carnatic in the summer of
1780, and were met by two British columns
of company troops from Madras and British
regulars. The British column of 4,000 men,
under the command of Lieutenant-Colonel
William Baillie, was defeated at the battle of
Pollimore on September 6, 1780. General Sir
Eyre Coote, hero of the battle of Wandiwash
and Commander-in-Chief in India, arrived
after the defeat with a significant
reinforcement of troops from the Bengal
Presidency. By the end of 1781, Coote had
defeated Haidar Ali's army at the battles of
Porto Novo on July 1, Polilur on August 27,
and Sholinghur on September 27. Even so,
Coote had failed to completely push Haidar
Ali out of the Carnatic. The British forces
lacked sufficient numbers of cavalry to drive
home their advantages.

The first actions of 1782 were undertaken
by the French, who landed three French
regular regiments at Porto Novo in aid of

Battle at St. Helier, Jersey. (Anne SK Brown Collection)

Haidar Ali on February 21. The fighting for the year was primarily carried on by the French and British fleets off the coast of the Carnatic and Ceylon, although the British garrison on Ceylon surrendered in August.

Haidar Ali died in late 1782, and his son, Tipu Sultan, took over command of the kingdom and army. Tipu returned to the Carnatic area, along with a second French force, which arrived at Porto Novo on March 16, 1783. The British, recognizing the danger, immediately set out to destroy the French regular forces and contingent of sepoys. The two armies met outside Cuddalore in June.

The French built a defended position, which the British attacked on June 13. The battle lasted all day, as a British observer noted: "The bloody contest continued without intermission until 5 o'clock in the evening when a cessation of firing took place … both lines were overcome with fatigue [thus they] lay upon their arms" (Munro, Narrative, p. 328). The French outer defenses

had been breached, but they withdrew safely to the town's walls. On June 25, the French launched an unsuccessful attack on the British siege lines. Both sides withdrew upon receiving the news that peace negotiations had begun back in Europe earlier in the year.

The war with Tipu continued into the following year, but ended eventually because Tipu could gain no further French support, leaving the British free to concentrate on his army. The Mysore Wars did not end officially until 1799, when Tipu's capital, Seringapatam, was taken and Tipu himself killed.

Peace

In February 1782, Lord Germain resigned as British Secretary of State for America. Lord North and his government resigned on March 20. The new government, led by the Marquis of Rockingham, took office. Rockingham's government wanted peace with the American colonies so that it could concentrate on the Bourbon menace, and in

June, Lieutenant-General Haldimand, Commander-in-Chief of Canada, was advised that all offensive operations against the Thirteen Colonies were to cease.

British and American negotiators began to meet during the summer of 1782. The negotiations lasted for five months, as the two sides worked out the boundaries of the new country and other relevant issues, such as fishing rights. The preliminary peace was formally established between the British and the new American government on November 30, 1782. Under its terms, the British accepted the independence of the United States; all British troops stationed in the United States would withdraw. The land between the Appalachian Mountains and the Mississippi River was given to the United States, and they also received access to George's Bank, the fishing grounds off Newfoundland. The United States agreed to honor debts accrued during the war and to treat loyalists fairly. Many loyalists, however, chose to leave the country and move to Canada, the West Indies, or Great Britain, not trusting their new government and fearful of the future. Orders arrived on July 14, 1782, for the British to evacuate Savannah; Charleston followed on December 18, 1782. New York was not formally evacuated until November 25, 1783.

The French and Spanish had made considerable progress in eradicating the humiliations of the Seven Years' War, but the war was becoming a stalemate, and all sides were weary of it. Preliminary peace talks began among the British, French, Spanish, and Dutch in late 1782. By January 1783, an armistice had been agreed and a preliminary peace treaty signed, although fighting continued in some regions too distant to hear immediately of the agreements.

The Treaty of Paris was signed on September 3, 1783. Britain handed over the Floridas (East and West) and Minorca to Spain, retaining Gibraltar and the Bahamas. France regained Senegal, St. Lucia, Tobago, and her interests in India, notably Pondicherry. The paucity of decisive naval victories for either side made it difficult to claim any major territorial gains. The British were able to retain possessions in the West Indies that they had held before the war began, and lost nothing in India.

Influence of the American Revolution

The American Revolution arose out of a dispute that began with Great Britain's change in policy toward her colonies. The trend toward a cohesive worldwide British empire, commercially and strategically powerful, was not checked by the outcome of the war. Rather, it meant that Britain shifted her focus from the Thirteen Colonies as the centerpiece of this empire, and began to concentrate on the potential of India instead. The drive for empire would shape the fate of Britain, and of most of the world, throughout the 19th century and beyond.

In the wake of defeat in North America, Britain was also forced to assess once again the strengths and weaknesses of her army and navy. This evaluation led to reforms, which prepared the British Army and Royal Navy for further conflict with France, Britain's traditional enemy, during the French Revolution and the reign of Napoleon.

As described above, France suffered economically from her participation in the war, even though she fought on the winning side. The debts incurred in supporting the Americans with money and arms contributed to the steadily worsening economic situation at home and are frequently cited as one of the root causes of the revolution that inflamed France only a few years later. There is a popular belief that the French Revolution was motivated by events in America, and it is ironic that this may be true, although not necessarily for the reasons commonly cited.

After the Treaty of Paris, the newborn United States of America was left independent and possessed of the rights for which she had fought—to trade freely, impose her own taxes, and determine her own military requirements. Possessed of a flourishing economy and boundless national resources, her opportunities appeared limitless. Indeed, the United States would succeed, with the help of liberal trade policies and the recruitment of successive waves of enthusiastic immigrants, in transforming itself into the most powerful English-speaking country on Earth in less than two centuries.

The infant nation was also left in 1783 with the delicate problem of bringing together 13 distinct entities with diverse and sometimes contradictory needs and views into a cohesive unit, and of reconciling the power of the local assemblies with the creation of an effective national representative government. The issue of where States' Rights ended and federal power began was the greatest consideration in structuring this new political entity. The decisions made concerning States' Rights, particularly with regard to the legality of slavery, were to have ramifications that would dominate the first hundred years of United States history. They culminated in a conflict that brought the young country to the brink of destruction: the War Between the States (the American Civil War) in the mid-19th century.

Glossary

autocratic Ruling with absolute power; having unlimited power over others.

boycott To join together in refusing to deal with, so as to punish; to refuse to buy, sell, or use.

cavalry Combat troops mounted on horses.

contingent A share or quota of troops; a group forming part of a larger group.

covert Concealed; hidden; disguised; secret.

defray To pay the money for the cost or expense of something.

dragoon A soldier armed with a short musket, capable of firing on horseback or on foot; a mounted infantryman or heavily armed cavalryman.

grievance A circumstance thought to be unjust or injurious and grounds for complaint or resentment; complaint, resentment, or statement expressing complaint or resentment over a real or imagined wrong.

incursion A sudden, brief invasion or raid.

infantry Foot soldiers; soldiers trained and equipped to fight on foot.

insurrection A rising up against established authority; rebellion; revolt.

irregular A soldier not belonging to a regularly established army.

linear Made of or using lines; extended in a line.

loyalist A person who supports the established government of his or her country during times of revolt; an American colonist loyal to the British government.

militia An army composed of citizens, rather than professional soldiers, called out in times of emergency.

odious Arousing or deserving hatred or loathing; disgusting; offensive.

propaganda The systematic, widespread dissemination or promotion of particular ideas, doctrines, allegations, or practices (which may in fact be deceitful or distorted) to further one's own cause or to damage an opposing one.

rabble A noisy, disorderly crowd; a mob.

regular A soldier belonging to the permanently constituted or standing army of a country.

skirmish A brief fight or encounter between small armed groups, usually as part of a larger battle; a slight, unimportant conflict.

For more information

American Independence Museum
One Governors Lane
Exeter, NH 03833
(603) 772-2622

Web site: http://www.
independencemuseum.org
Located in historic Exeter, New Hampshire,
the museum features stories of the brave

men and women who overcame their uncertainties about freedom from Great Britain and established a new, independent country. The American Independence Museum's exhibits highlight the Society of the Cincinnati, the nation's oldest veterans' society, and its first president, George Washington. Among the museum's permanent collection of documents chronicling the nation's founding are an original Dunlap Broadside of the Declaration of Independence and early drafts of the U.S. Constitution. Permanent collections include American furnishings, ceramics, silver, textiles, and military ephemera.

Daughters of the American Revolution (DAR)
National Society
1776 D Street NW
Washington, DC 20006-5303
(202) 628-1776
Web site: http://www.dar.org/museum
The DAR, founded in 1890 and headquartered in Washington, D.C., is a nonprofit, nonpolitical volunteer women's service organization dedicated to promoting patriotism, preserving American history, and securing America's future through better education for children. DAR National Headquarters houses one of the nation's premier genealogical libraries, one of the foremost collections of pre-industrial American decorative arts, Washington's largest concert hall, and an extensive collection of early American manuscripts and imprints. The DAR Museum is comprised of thirty-one period rooms and two galleries. Its collection consists of over 30,000 decorative and fine arts objects spanning the eighteenth and nineteenth centuries, including furniture, glass, ceramics, textiles, and silver.

Fraunces Tavern Museum
54 Pearl Street
New York, NY 10004
(212) 425-1776

Web site: http://www.frauncestavernmuseum.org
Though it is best known as the site where Washington gave his farewell address to the officers of the Continental Army in 1783, Fraunces Tavern also played a significant role in pre-Revolutionary activities. After the war, when New York was the nation's first capital, the tavern was rented to the new government to house the offices of the Departments of War, Treasury, and Foreign Affairs. In 1904, the Sons of the Revolution in the State of New York purchased the tavern and hired preservation architect William Mersereau to return the building to its colonial appearance. Fraunces Tavern® Museum opened to the public in 1907. Today, the museum complex includes four nineteenth-century buildings in addition to the eighteenth-century Fraunces Tavern building. Fraunces Tavern® Museum's mission is to educate the public about New York City history as it relates to colonial America, the Revolutionary War, and the Early Republic. This mission is fulfilled through the preservation and interpretation of the museum's landmarked 1719 building along with varied exhibitions of art and artifacts as they relate to the historic site.

Independence National Historical Park
143 South Third Street
Philadelphia, PA 19106
(800) 537-7676
Web site: http://www.nps.gov
The park contains both Independence Hall and the Liberty Bell Center. From 1775 to 1783, Independence Hall was the meeting place for the Second Continental Congress. It was in the Assembly Room of this building that George Washington was appointed Commander-in-Chief of the Continental Army in 1775 and the Declaration of Independence was adopted on July 4, 1776. In the same room the design of the American flag was agreed

upon in 1777, the Articles of Confederation were adopted in 1781, and the U.S. Constitution was drafted in 1787.

National Archives and Records Administration
8601 Adelphi Road
College Park, MD 20740-6001
Web site: http://www.archives.gov
The National Archives and Records Administration (NARA) is the nation's record keeper. The Archives house the Declaration of Independence, the Articles of Confederation, the Constitution, the Bill of Rights, the Emancipation Proclamation, the Louisiana Purchase agreement, along with other documents of national importance like military and immigration records, and even the Apollo 11 flight plan. Archives locations in fourteen cities, from coast-to-coast, protect and provide public access to millions of records.

National Museum of the American Revolution
Washington Crossing State Park
355 Washington Crossing-Pennington Road
Titusville, NJ 08560
Web site: http://www. nationalmuseumoftheamericanrevolution.org
The online museum and "brick-and-mortar" artifact collection are devoted to telling the story of the American Revolution.

Sons of the American Revolution National Society
1000 South Fourth Street
Louisville, KY 40203
(502) 589-1776
Web site: http://www.sar.org
The Sons of the American Revolution perpetuates the ideals of the war for independence. As a historical, educational, patriotic, and nonprofit corporation, it seeks to maintain and expand the meaning of patriotism, respect for national symbols, the value of American citizenship, and the unifying force of "e pluribus unum" that was created from the people of many nations—one nation and one people.

Valley Forge National Historic Park
1400 North Outer Line Drive
King of Prussia, PA 19406
(610) 783-1077
Web site: http://www.nps.gov/vafo
Valley Forge is the site of the 1777–78 winter encampment of the Continental Army. The park commemorates the sacrifices and perseverance of the Revolutionary War generation and honors the ability of citizens to pull together and overcome adversity during extraordinary times.

Washington Crossing Historic Park
Box 103
Washington Crossing, PA 18977
(215) 493-4076
Web site: http://www.ushistory.org/ washingtoncrossing
Washington Crossing Historic Park preserves and interprets for citizens and visitors the site at which General George Washington planned and executed his daring crossing of the Delaware River on December 25, 1776, leading to victory in the Battle of Trenton and turning the tide of the Revolutionary War. The park also honors and preserves the social and economic history of this important location.

Web sites

Due to the changing nature of Internet links, Rosen Publishing has developed an online list of Web sites related to the subject of this book. This site is updated regularly. Please use this link to access the list:

http://www.rosenlinks.com/eaw/rev

For further reading

Primary sources

Manuscript sources
The British Library
Lord Auckland Papers
Haldimand Papers
Hardwicke Papers
Munro Collection
Add. Mss. 32413   Lt. William Digby Journal
Add. Mss. 32627   Journal of Alescambe
   Chesney
Add. Mss. 57715   Siege of Charleston
Add. Mss. 57716   Siege of Savannah

National Army Museum
5701-9   Accounts of Brandywine,
   Germantown, and the siege of Gibraltar
7204-6-4   Letters of Lord Howe, General
   Burgoyne, and Lord George Germain
8010-32   Nicaragua Expedition
8010-32-1   Lieutenant-Colonel Stephen
   Kemble
8010-32-3   Major James MacDonald

Public Records Office, Kew
Amherst Papers
Cornwallis Papers

Boston Public Library, Manuscript Division
Ch.B. 12.72   Diary of an American soldier,
   4/19/1775-5/13/1775
Ch.F.7.78   Major-General Frederick von
   Steuben Militia Rules
Ch.F.7.85   General Putnam's condemnation
Ch.F.8.55a   Lieutenant-Colonel Jean
   Baptiste Tennant's comments on the
   Continental Army
G.33.10   Diary of American Service at
   Quebec and Saratoga
G.33.37   Salem Selectmen
G.380   Major-General Benjamin Lincoln
   Papers
G.380.20   Journal Siege of Charleston

Ms.R.1.4   General Orders for British Army,
   1775
Ms.9.AM   General Orders for the British
   Army during Yorktown Campaign
Mss. Acc. 568   Benjamin Gould
Mss. Acc. 1328   Commission for Alexander
   Innes as Inspector-General of Loyalist
   Troops, 1777

Massachusetts Historical Society, Boston
Isaac Bangs Journal
Nathaniel Ober Diary
Samuel Shaw Papers

The Bostonian Society
Doc. 973.38   Letter of Rev. John Tucker, 1768

Printed sources
Allaire, A., *Diary of Anthony Allaire*, New
   York, 1968.
Anburey, T., *With Burgoyne from Quebec: An
   Account of the Life at Quebec and of the
   Famous Battle at Saratoga*, Toronto, 1963.
Andre, J., *Major Andre's Journal: Operations of
   the British Army Under Lieut. Generals Sir
   William Howe and Sir Henry Clinton*,
   Tarrytown, New York, 1930.
Balderston, M., and D. Syrett, *The Lost War:
   Letters from British Officers During the
   American Revolution*, New York, 1975.
Barker, J., *The British in Boston: Being a Diary
   of Lt. John Barker*, Cambridge, Mass., 1924.
Barrett, A., *The Concord Fight: An Account*,
   Boston, Mass., 1901.
Clinton, H., *The American Rebellion: Sir Henry
   Clinton's Narrative of His Campaigns,
   1775–1782*, New Haven, Conn., 1954.
Closen, L., *The Revolutionary Journal of Baron
   Ludwig von Closen*, Chapel Hill, NC, 1958.
Collins, V., (ed), *A Brief Narrative of the
   Ravages of the British and Hessians at
   Princeton in 1775–1776*, Princeton,
   NJ, 1906.

Dearborn, H., *Revolutionary War Journals of Henry Dearborn*, New York, 1969.

Deux-Ponts, C., *My Campaign in America: Journal Kept by Count William de Deux-Ponts*, Boston, Mass., 1868.

Evelyn, W., *Memoir and Letters of Captain W. Glanville Evelyn of the 4th Regiment*, Oxford, 1879.

Ewald, J., *Diary of the American War: A Hessian Journal*, New Haven, Conn., 1979.

Fletcher, E., *The Narrative of Ebenezer Fletcher*, New York, 1970.

Greenman, J., *Diary of a Common Soldier in the American Revolution, 1775–1783*, DeKalb, Ill., 1978.

Hadden, J., *Hadden's Journal and Orderly Books: A Journal Kept in Canada and Upon Burgoyne's March*, Albany, New York, 1884.

Haskell, C., *Diary of Caleb Haskell*, Newburyport, Mass., 1881.

Hulton, A., *Letters of a Loyalist Lady*, Cambridge, Mass., 1927.

Jones, C., (ed), *Siege of Savannah by Count D'Estaing*, New York, 1968.

Kemble, S., *Journals of Lieutenant-Colonel Stephen Kemble and British Army Orders 1775–1778*, Boston, Mass., 1972.

Lister, J., *The Concord Fight: Narrative of Ensign Jeremy Lister*, Cambridge, Mass., 1931.

London Gazette, 1775–83.

Mackenzie, F., *Diary of Frederick Mackenzie: Being a Daily Narrative of His Military Service*, 2 vols, Cambridge, Mass., 1930.

Martin, J., *Private Yankee Doodle Dandee: Being a Narrative of Some of the Adventures, Dangers, and Sufferings, of a Revolutionary Soldier*, Boston, Mass., 1962.

Military Guide for Young Officers containing a System of the Art of War, London, 1776.

Moultrie, W., *Memoirs of the American Revolution So Far as it Related to the States of North and South Carolina and Georgia*, 2 vols, New York, 1802.

Munro, I., *The Munro Letters*, Liverpool, 1988.

Munro, I., *Narrative of the Military Operations on the Coromandel Coast Against the Combined Forces of the French, Dutch, and Hyder Ally*, London, 1789.

Planches Relatives à l'Exercise de L'infanterie suivant L'Ordinnace du Roi du premier Juin 1776, Lille, 1776.

Recicourt, L., "American Revolutionary Army: A French Estimate in 1777," *Military Analysis of the American Revolutionary War*, Millwodd, New York, 1977.

Regulations for the Order and Discipline of the Troops of the United States, Philadelphia, Penn., 1779.

Rice, H., and A. S. K. Brown, (eds), *The American Campaigns of Rochambeau's Army*, 2 vols, Princeton, NJ, and Providence, RI, 1972.

Saavedra, D., *Journal of Don Francisco Saavedra de Sangronis During the Commission Which He Had in His Charge from 1780 Until 1783*, Gainesville, Fla, 1989.

Scheer, G., and H. Rankin, *Rebels and Redcoats*, New York, 1957.

Simcoe, J., *Journal of the Operations of the Queen's Rangers, from the End of the Year 1777 to the Conclusion of the Late American War*, Exeter, 1787.

Tallmadge, B., *Memoir of Colonel Benjamin Tallmadge*, New York, 1858.

Tarleton, B., *A History of the Campaigns of 1780 and 1781, in the Southern Provinces of North America*, London, 1787.

Uhlendorf, B., trans., *Revolution in America: Confidential Letters and Journals 1776–1784 of Adjutant General Major Baurmeister of the Hessian Troops*, New Brunswick, NJ, 1957.

Uhlendorf, B., trans., *The Siege of Charleston: Diaries and Letters of Hessian Officers*, Ann Arbor, Mich., 1938.

Wright, E., *Fire of Liberty*, New York, 1983.

Secondary sources

Allen, R. S., *Loyal Americans: The Military Role of the Provincial Corps*, Ottawa, 1983.

Atwood, R., *The Hessians*, Cambridge, Mass., 1980.

Black, J., *War for America: The Fight for Independence*, Stroud, 1991.

Bowler, R. A., *Logistics and the Failure of the British Army in America*, Princeton, NJ, 1975.

Christie, I., and B. Labaree, *Empire or Independence*, Oxford, 1976.

Conway, S., *The War of American Independence*, London, 1995.

Curtis, E., *The Organization of the British Army in the American Revolution*, New Haven, Conn., 1926.

Duffy, C., *The Military Experience in the Age of Reason*, New York, 1988.

Dull, J., *A Diplomatic History of the American Revolution*, New Haven, Conn., 1985.

Dull, J., *The French Navy and American Independence: A Study of Arms and Diplomacy, 1775–1787*, Princeton, NJ, 1975.

Higginbottom, D., *War and Society in Revolutionary America*, Columbia, SC, 1988.

Higginbottom, D., *The War of American Independence: Military Attitudes, Policies, and Practices 1763–1789*, New York, 1971.

Houlding, J. A., *Fit for Service: Training of the British Army*, Oxford, 1981.

Kennett, L., *French Forces in America*, Westport, Conn., 1977.

Lynch, J., *Bourbon Spain 1700–1808*, Oxford, 1989.

Mackesy, P., *War for America*, 2nd edition, London, 1993.

Marston, J. G., *King and Congress the Transfer of Political Legitimacy, 1774–1776*, Princeton, N.J, c. 1987.

Nordholt, J. W. S., *The Dutch Republic and American Independence*, Chapel Hill, NC, 1982.

Royster, C., *A Revolutionary People at War: The Continental Army and American Character*, Chapel Hill, NC, 1979.

Shy, J., *A People Numerous and Armed: Reflections on the Military Struggle for American Independence*, Oxford, 1976.

Smith, P. H., *Loyalists and Redcoats: A Study in British Revolutionary Policy*, Chapel Hill, NC, 1964.

Syrett, D., *The Royal Navy in American Waters*, Aldershot, 1989.

Weigley, R., *Towards an American Army*, New York, 1962.

Wright, R. K., *The Continental Army*, Washington, DC, 1983.

Index

About the authors

Professor Robert O'Neill is the series editor of Early American Wars. His wealth of knowledge and expertise shapes the series content and provides up-to-the-minute research and theory. Born in 1936 an Australian citizen, he served in the Australian army (1955–68) and has held a number of eminent positions in history circles, including the Chichele Professorship of the History of War at All Souls College, University of Oxford, 1987–2001, and the Chairmanship of the Board of the Imperial War Museum and the Council of the International Institute for Strategic Studies, London, England. He is the author of many

books, including works on the German army and the Nazi party, and the Korean and Vietnam wars. Now based in Australia on his retirement from Oxford, he is the Chairman of the Council of the Australian Strategic Policy Institute.

Daniel Marston completed both his BA and MA in History at McGill University, Montreal, Canada, and his DPhil in the History of War at Balliol College, Oxford. His book *The Seven Years' War* was published in 2001. Daniel was born and raised in Boston, Massachusetts, and now lives in Dorchester, Massachusetts.

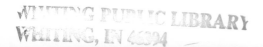